TRUTH, LIFE, THE CHURCH, AND THE GOSPEL —

THE FOUR GREAT PILLARS IN THE LORD'S RECOVERY

WITNESS LEE

Living Stream Ministry

Anaheim, CA • www.lsm.org

First Edition, January 2002.

ISBN 978-0-7363-1561-6

Published by

Living Stream Ministry
2431 W. La Palma Ave., Anaheim, CA 92801 U.S.A.
P. O. Box 2121, Anaheim, CA 92814 U.S.A.

Printed in the United States of America

14 15 16 17 18 19 / 10 9 8 7 6 5 4 3 2

CONTENTS

PREFACE

This book is composed of messages given by Brother Witness Lee in meetings for elders and co-workers and in a conference held in Manila, Philippines in November 1984.

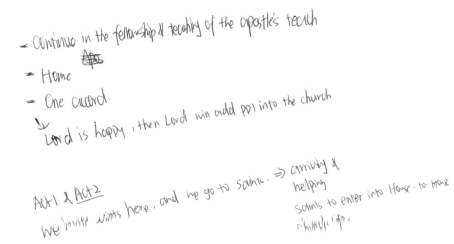

CHAPTER ONE

THE WAY TO KNOW THE BIBLE

The Lord has raised up His recovery upon the truth. Over the past years, the Lord in His recovery has completed the life-study of the entire New Testament and the life-studies of Genesis and Exodus in the Old Testament. This is the precious inheritance that the Lord has given to His recovery. We should enter into all the truths of the Bible by means of the life-study messages. We should not merely obtain some enjoyment from them; rather, we should gain some practical knowledge and experience.

HOW TO USE THE LIFE-STUDIES

The Bible is a special work of literature. Although it does not focus on any particular topic, it has a central theme that is comprehensive, encompassing many matters. Over the ages, the greatest difficulty for Bible readers has been the difficulty of seeing the Bible's central light and the comprehensiveness of its light. Thus, their understanding of the Bible has been fragmented and peripheral. They may have understood a point here and a point there, but they have not been able to gain a complete understanding. If we want to have a complete understanding of the Bible, we must see that the Bible has only one center and that this center encompasses many matters; it is comprehensive.

Under this principle the life-studies have a center. They also contain explanations and definitions of various matters, so they are comprehensive as well. Therefore, when we study the life-studies, we are always able to obtain the life nourishment from them, and we are also able to gain some knowledge of the truth. However, because they are comprehensive and are not focused on one specific topic, it is difficult for people to see the center. This is why when we study the life-studies with people, we must point out the central theme and present the main points to them.

Pointing Out the Central Theme and All of Its Aspects

Let us take the *Life-study of Exodus* as an example. All Bible students know that Exodus speaks of Christ and that Christ is the center of Exodus. However, to know this in such a simple way is insufficient. First, we must point out which aspects of Christ are spoken of in Exodus. Then we should point out how Exodus presents all these aspects of Christ. Some people say that Exodus speaks about matters such as the death of Christ and the resurrection of Christ. This kind of answer is very general and does not reveal to us in a practical way the reality we see and enjoy in Exodus. For example, someone may ask you what you had for dinner, and you may answer in a definite way that you ate fish, shrimp, meat, tofu, and fruit. In the same way, we must be able to point out how Exodus speaks about the death of Christ and His resurrection. Only by doing this will we be able to show forth all the aspects of Christ.

The central theme of Exodus is how Christ becomes everything to us. First, He became our Passover Lamb. The blood of the Passover lamb typifies the precious blood of Christ shed for the forgiveness of our sins (Matt. 26:28; John 19:34; 1 Pet. 1:18-19). There is also the meat which typifies the generating life of Christ as our supply (John 6:53, 55). Then there is the unleavened bread that typifies Christ Jesus who is our nourishment of life and who takes away all our sinful and evil things (1 Cor. 5:7-8). Finally there are the bitter herbs that indicate that we need to regret and repent, to experience bitterness in the matter of sinful things.

When we consider this picture, we can see that there is a relationship between eating and living. If we want to live, we must eat; if we do not eat, we cannot live. The Lord Jesus said, "He who eats Me, he also shall live because of Me" (John 6:57). The first "meal" presented to us in Exodus is the Passover.

This meal indicates that Christ shed His precious blood for the forgiveness of sins and that His life enters into us as our supply and nourishment to enable us to give up all sinful things. Moreover, when we sin, we experience a bitter feeling that causes us to repent of our sins.

Then, when the Israelites left Egypt, God gave them the heavenly food—manna, which typifies Christ as the heavenly life supply to be our daily nourishment and satisfaction that causes us to live by Him (John 6:31-35, 48-51, 57-58). Later, God led the Israelites to experience the water flowing from the cleft rock. Paul said that the Israelites "all drank the same spiritual drink; for they drank of a spiritual rock which followed them, and the rock was Christ" (1 Cor. 10:4). This living water typifies the Spirit who flows from the crucified and resurrected Christ as the all-inclusive water to supply us (John 7:37-39; 1 Cor. 12:13). Christ is also the tabernacle of God, that is, the dwelling place of God and the dwelling place of us, the priests. We can abide in Him, enjoying the inward supply of the golden lampstand, the table of the bread of the Presence, and the golden incense altar. These are all types of Christ.

Checking These Types with Our Practical Experience and Applying Them to Our Daily Living

These items added together are comprehensive and not limited to one aspect. Furthermore, they can be checked with our Christian experience. First, we have the precious blood of Christ that washes us from our sins. The New Testament clearly says that the blood of Jesus, God's Son, cleanses us from every sin (1 John 1:7). Next, Christ dispenses His life into us; in a sense, this is for us to eat Him. The meat of the lamb was distributed to all the people, and if anyone did not eat, he did not partake of the rich supply of Christ the Lamb.

The matter of eating the Lord is truly a great gospel. Unfortunately, today's Christians almost never speak of eating the Lord, and they even oppose this matter because they think, "How can we eat the Lord?" The Bible, however, clearly says that the Lord wants us to eat Him (John 6:53-57). The

Old Testament is a picture in which God did not want the Israelites just to eat the meat of the lamb but also to eat the unleavened bread and the bitter herbs with it. This signifies that when we eat the Lord as our enjoyment, we must get rid of all our sinful things; this is the experience of the unleavened bread. Simultaneously, He joins Himself to us inwardly, causing us to feel that we are corrupted and to become inwardly sorrowful; this is the experience of the bitter herbs. These are all practical matters of enjoyment to us.

If we only read about the types and study the doctrines without comparing them to our own experiences, it will not be easy to understand Exodus. However, if we compare our experiences to these types, they are very easy to understand because they are descriptions of our normal Christian living. For example, when we Christians get up early in the morning to read the Bible and pray, this is our eating the manna. However, the manna cannot be eaten carelessly. The picture in the Old Testament shows us that there are definite rules for gathering the manna. First, the manna had to be gathered every morning (Exo. 16:21). Some people might have been lazy and reluctant to rise early in the morning, so they did not gather the manna and were hungry all day. Second, the manna could not be kept until the next day (v. 19). Some people were greedy and gathered large piles of manna which they were unable to finish eating, and the next day the manna bred worms and stank (v. 20). According to our experience, the matter of gathering the manna indicates first of all that we must spend time every morning to read the Lord's Word and to draw near to Him; otherwise, we will not be able to obtain each day's supply of life. Second, it indicates that the supply of life is for our enjoyment for one day only and cannot be kept over to the next day.

Through the principle of gathering the manna we see God's balancing hand. Even though God did not allow the people to gather a double portion of manna each day, He gave them two days' worth of manna on the sixth day of the week in order to enable them to keep the Sabbath on the seventh day. That extra portion did not breed worms but provided them with fresh enjoyment. This indicates that the enjoyment of Christ is not according to our method or calculation; rather, it is according to God's ordination and arrangement. Let us also check the type of the tabernacle with our experience of abiding in the Lord. Christ is the tabernacle of God, the dwelling place of God, and He is also our dwelling place. In the tabernacle are the golden lampstand, the bread of the Presence, and the golden incense altar. When we abide in the Lord, we obtain the supply of the bread of the Presence, receive the enlightening of the golden lampstand, and enjoy Him as our acceptable incense offered to God.

Apprehending and Experiencing All the Aspects of Christ

Exodus does not use any clear terms referring to Christ's death. However, with the help of the life-study messages we can clearly see that although Exodus does not use the word *death* to talk about Christ's death, it does use the killing of the Passover lamb to describe Christ's death. In addition, while the Passover lamb does not directly show the resurrection of Christ, the lamb actually implies the reality of Christ's resurrection. The meat of the lamb eventually entered into its eaters to be their life supply. This implies the process of resurrection. Christ can be received into us to supply us inwardly and to live in us; this implies that He has gone through the process of death and resurrection. Therefore, the precious blood refers to the aspect of Christ's death, and the meat of the lamb entering into the Israelites refers to the aspect of resurrection. The blood was spread on the doorposts and on the lintel, signifying the crucified Christ as our covering. The meat was eaten to get into the people, signifying the resurrected Christ entering into us as our spiritual supply. This is our experience of the crucified and resurrected Christ.

Moreover, Exodus does not use the specific term *ascension* to refer to the ascension of Christ, nor does it tell us where Christ went after He ascended, but this matter is implied in the manna. Manna came down from heaven to the Israelites, signifying Christ coming down from heaven as food for God's people. Moreover, manna came from God and descended from heaven, implying that when Christ ascended, He ascended to God, that is, to the Father (John 20:17).

The Passover is a very clear picture showing the killing of the Passover lamb as a type of Christ's death and the shedding of His precious blood that washes us of all our sins and becomes our covering.) It also shows the Israelites eating the meat of the lamb and taking it into them as a type of the resurrected Christ as our life supply. Finally, it shows the manna coming down from heaven as a type of Christ's ascending to the highest heaven and descending again to be our daily life supply. This is our experience of the ascended Christ.

ENTERING INTO THE TRUTHS OF THE BIBLE THROUGH THE LIFE-STUDY MESSAGES

Some criticize us, saying that we read the life-study messages and not the Bible. Those who speak this way are completely misinformed. The goal of the life-study messages is to bring people into the truths of the Bible. In the past when people read the Bible, they could not find the way to enter in, so they had no way to understand it. This is like having a house with no entryway, no door, and no windows to allow people to enter in) The life-study messages do the work of paving a way, building a door, and opening a window so that people can enter the house and enjoy everything inside.

THE LIFE-STUDY MESSAGES LEADING PEOPLE TO TOUCH LIFE

Another function of the life-study messages is to bring people into life. The life-study messages are not a set of philosophical or classical writings apart from the Bible. The life-study messages do not merely expound the Bible and present the truth; rather, they also bring people into the truth to enjoy and experience its riches. Mere exposition of the Bible is just the impartation of knowledge which causes people to know doctrines mentally. The life-study messages bring us into the depths of the Bible to touch and enjoy the life within (cf. John 5:39-40).

Many Christians after reading Exodus 12 only know that something happened on the night of the Passover (v. 12); they do not know the meaning of what happened. However, today through the life-study messages we can all understand the deep meaning of this matter and enter into the application of the precious blood, the enjoyment of the meat of the lamb, and the reality of the unleavened bread and bitter herbs. Therefore, the life-study of the Bible is a proper and accurate study of the Bible which ushers people into the Bible to obtain the life supply and enjoyment contained in it.

THE FACTOR FOR RICH MEETINGS

Today pastors and preachers in Christianity must search everywhere to find a good word for their sermons. Some pastors do not have anything to talk about, so they speak about things such as sanitary practices and personal hygiene. Some are a little better and speak about matters such as redemption, the washing away of sins, and justification. There are some who are even deeper and speak about things such as how to fellowship with the Lord and how to enjoy the peace given to us by the Lord. But even this is not really enough when we speak of the richness of the meetings. We have seen from our experience and our research that the richest meetings are those with the life-study messages as their content. If every Lord's Day we would take two life-study messages as the content of our fellowship, the meeting would be very rich.

I personally have spent eleven years laboring to carry out the summer and winter life-study trainings. This year I have completed the life-study of the entire New Testament, and next year I will begin another eleven years to complete the study of the entire Bible. We should bring all the saints in the churches in the Lord's recovery into the practice of carefully reading one or two life-study messages each week. If we do this, over the long term—perhaps over ten, eight, or even just five years—the saints will make much progress in all areas, and the condition of the entire church will also be reversed.

Nutritionists tell us that to eat healthily, we cannot eat just one kind of food. Fish is very nutritious, but if we only ate fish for three meals a day without eating anything else, we definitely would not be healthy. In order to eat healthily, we must eat all kinds of foods. For example, a salad does not contain only one kind of vegetable but many kinds mixed together; thus, salads are rich and nutritious. The life-study messages are like a salad that is made not with just one kind of vegetable but with all different kinds. However, we must have our staple food, our center. Christ as life is the center of the life-study messages, so when we read the life-study messages, they help us to grow strong and healthy in life.

Before 1974, we mainly emphasized releasing messages on one topic at a time through conferences. Later we realized that we should dig out the matter of life because life is the center. So from that time on, we began to dig out life from the Bible, book by book through the life-study messages. At present, we have dug out life from each book of the New Testament and even the Old Testament books of Genesis and Exodus. Although the Bible was written comprehensively, speaking much on many topics, it always has life as its center to clearly point out the way.

Even the short book of Ephesians with only six chapters is composed in a comprehensive way, speaking on many topics. For example, the book of Ephesians speaks of very high matters—matters which could not be any higher—such as God's selection in eternity and His predestinating us (1:4-5). It also speaks of very low matters—matters which could not be any lower—as in the word that those who steal should steal no more (4:28). If today we were to choose a topic and speak of God's calling and predestination, we would not also speak of such things as stealing. However, after the book of Ephesians speaks of such high matters, it suddenly inserts just such a sentence, telling those who steal to steal no more. It also tells the husbands to love their wives and tells the wives to submit to their husbands (5:25, 22). This proves that the Bible's way of speaking is comprehensive. Nevertheless, the Bible still has its center. When we use the life-study messages, we must firmly grasp this point and see that the Bible has an intrinsic central lane and also speaks comprehensively on many matters.

CONSTANTLY MAKING PROGRESS IN THE TRUTH

Some people have said that in the life-study messages there are many new, deep terms that are hard for ordinary saints to understand. In recent years American educators have discovered that as our era progresses, the knowledge of our children progresses along with it. The things that we thought children would not understand are now easy for them to understand. The things which children are able to understand according to their intelligence far surpass the contents of their textbooks. For example, computer classes are now beginning to be taught in elementary school, so many households are buying computers for children under the age of ten to practice on and use. This is worth our consideration.

The principle is the same in considering the development of Christianity in China. The first step was taken when the Western missionaries spoke messages about joy and peace in order to get people to accept their preaching. They told people that as soon as they believed in God they would be blessed, obtain profit, and enjoy peace. This kind of speaking at the very beginning matched people's psychology, because in this world the human life is mainly a life of suffering and troubles, and everyone wants blessings, prosperity, and peace. Actually, people can understand this kind of preaching without any explanation. It is preached for the purpose of lifting people's hearts and producing a desire and willingness to believe in the Lord Jesus for the forgiveness of sins, the obtaining of peace, and the enjoyment of God's blessing. However, if we stop there, after a long time man's heart will become cold. This is why those missionaries gradually improved their speaking and spoke about some basic truths in the Bible, telling people that there is one God who is the holy and righteous One and that this One sent His only begotten Son to shed His blood and die for us to redeem us from our sins and to save us from eternal perdition into eternal life. Today this is where many Christians have stopped.

There are, however, many deep truths in the Bible. The fourteen Epistles of Paul alone have many deep and high truths. For example, Ephesians 1:10 says, "Unto the economy of the fullness of the times, to head up all things in Christ, the things in the heavens and the things on the earth, in Him." It is very hard to understand this kind of word, but over the past twenty to thirty years the Lord has revealed to us these deep, high truths in the Bible. Our knowledge of the truth has not only been constantly progressing, but the younger we are, the more room there is for progress.

When computers first entered the homes, many among the older generation did not understand anything and could only listen to their grandchildren talk about computers. In the end they were still confused about things like software and hardware. Then one day the grandchildren turned on the computer in front of the older ones and demonstrated as they played, explaining what software is and what hardware is. Thus, the older ones were able to understand through the practical teaching of the grandchildren. In the same way we in the Lord's recovery should have a change in our concepts about the truth. We must not remain stuck in our old ways.

Items such as God's economy, God's dispensing, the essential Spirit, and the economical Spirit are certainly very deep terms, but to the new believers, especially the young ones, they will not seem deep for very long. These new ones will gradually become familiar with the terms, and then they will clearly understand them. We must be willing to change our concepts and must encourage the young ones to learn the highest and deepest truths. I believe that if we do so, in the future when the saints speak to each other and even when they preach the gospel, their speaking will be of the very highest quality. We will not need to charge them to preach the high gospel instead of the gospel of prosperity and peace. As soon as they open their mouths, the high truths will spontaneously come out. Today we may feel that this is not so easy, but very soon they will be using the terms *the essential Spirit* and *the economical Spirit* when they preach the gospel to others. The saints just need to be able to simply say, "Friend, we all are sinners; we all need the essential Spirit to get into us and regenerate us, giving us an inward change in our element. Moreover, God will also give us the economical Spirit so that we may be full of power in our living and actions." Do not think that people will not understand this word. Actually, we are the ones who do not understand it, so we think others will be just like us.

LEARNING TO SPEAK THE PROFOUND TRUTHS

We all know that in a child's learning process the child needs his parents to constantly give him input. For example, when he learns about love or smiling, the parents must keep telling him on the one hand and demonstrating to him on the other until he gradually understands the concept. Sometimes the parents must speak about things many times before the child can understand what they mean. Thus, learning comes from hearing. From now on, regardless of whether we are preaching the gospel or speaking God's word, we should not be afraid that people will not understand when we speak the profound truths. We must realize that these truths are actually what touch people the most.

Moreover, in a way it does not matter whether we speak something deep or shallow. The most important point is that we must learn the secret, the practical technique, of speaking. If we do not have the technique or secret, people will not understand us even when we speak the shallowest truths. If we learn the secret, we will be able to use very simple words to speak the deepest matters, and we will be able to bring people into spiritual reality. For example, when learning to use the computer, we cannot just have empty knowledge but must also pick up the right techniques. Then, when a computer is placed before us, we will know how to set it up, operate it, use it, and even teach others.

The Lord's recovery has the highest truths. Thus, if we learn the techniques, when we preach the gospel to people, we will be able to appropriately use the highest truths in the Lord's recovery and say, "Friend, we are all sinners without God inside of us. We do not have the nature of God, but as soon as we repent of our sins and turn to Him, God's essential Spirit enters into us, causing us to be regenerated and have God's life and nature. This is God's entering into us as our essence. Even more than this, after we are regenerated, if we are willing to deal with our sins and apply the Lord's blood for a thorough washing, then God's economical Spirit will be poured out upon us, making us full of power." I believe that anyone who hears such a word will be able to understand it. When new believers enter into the church life, if they are taught in this way, they will be able to quickly understand the proper meaning of each spiritual term, and they will be able to apply each one practically in their daily lives.

I hope that the standard of truth will be constantly raised higher among the churches in the Lord's recovery. We cannot remain in the shallow gospel truths such as peace and prosperity, Christ's incarnation to save sinners, His crucifixion to accomplish redemption, and God's love for the world. Although these things are right, they are still elementary, basic, and beginning truths. We must go up to the high peak. It is just like in the elementary schools today, where what they are teaching is much higher than what was taught ten or twenty years ago. Yet the children are still able to learn these things because the entire standard has been uplifted. Even in the daily conversation in the homes we can find that the standard among the children has been raised; many of them use terms in a familiar way that we never understood when we were young. In the same way, when many people were young, they did not understand such truths as the essential Spirit, the economical Spirit, or the dispensing of the Triune God, but now the young people all speak about these things, and their speaking is true and logical. This is what it means when people say that the students can go farther than the teachers.

May we all be able to really perfect the young people in the truth and encourage them to enter into the depths of the Lord's word. This is why we have a burden to recommend and promote the life-study messages. I hope that we would all be able to study and apply them and that we would teach the young people well so that they would receive the real help. If we do this, the Lord's recovery will have a wonderful future.

CHAPTER TWO

THE CHURCH AS THE GARDEN OF GOD

Our goal is to be a organic garden

THE CHURCH BEING A GARDEN
FULL OF ORGANIC FUNCTIONS

The church is like a garden. As Paul said, our work in the church is that of planting and watering while God alone causes the growth (1 Cor. 3:6-7). Furthermore, the church is not an organization but a living organism. The past condition of a church in a locality cannot be compared with its present condition because the church is an organism with organic functions and the ability to grow.

What is it to have an organic function? Suppose there is a table here with a chair next to it and with a cup on top of it. These three things would never generate any kind of organic function. They would remain in the same position after one year, three years, or even ten years. Nothing would grow from them; rather, they would become dirtier, older, more faded, and less attractive. This is because the table, the chair, and the cup do not have any organic function. However, suppose there is an orchard that has just been planted with tree seedlings. At first these seedlings may seem quite small and unsightly, almost ready to wither, yet after exposure to the sun and the rain, these unsightly fruit trees start to grow and even bring forth fruit. This is the inherent organic function of fruit trees.

Generally speaking, organic functions need to be developed. The seedlings may not be very evident in the first couple of years, but they will be manifested by the third year. After a while the formerly unsightly, small tree seedlings will grow quite big and tall and will begin to produce fruit. Even though initially they might have looked like they were about to die, eventually they will be so living and exuberant. Initially there might not have been even a single leaf, but eventually they will be full of green leaves. This kind of situation fills us with joy. The reason for our joy is that the manifestation of the organic functions fills us with hope.

A HISTORY OF THE LORD'S RECOVERY IN MANILA

When I came to Manila thirty years ago, the situation was completely different from the present situation. At that time the church life was not very active. I could not see much fruit being produced, nor could I see the organic functions being manifested in the services. Under God's sovereignty, He arranged for me to come here and to have three groups of people contact me. The first group was a group of eight to nine elders. One brother took the lead to tell me that both the church and the work had not been built up. Therefore, he said that they would like to hand over the church completely to me for me to take the lead.

The second group was a group of eight to nine co-workers, who were represented by a senior co-worker. He told me that the work here had never been built up and that they were ashamed of this. Therefore, he was representing the co-workers in their desire to place the work under my leadership. On the same night, all the deacons and deaconesses gathered at a sister's home. They sent a brother as their representative to tell me that they had not been serving properly in the church and that they too would like to hand over to me the service of the church for me to take the lead. These three groups of people, in three separate places and times, expressed the same desire.

After a couple of weeks on December 31, the end of that year, I called for a meeting and gathered these three groups of people together. In the meeting I said to them, "I have been here for one and a half months. The elders, co-workers, and deacons have all said to me that they want to hand over to me the church, the work, and the service here for me to take the lead. When we are sent by the Lord to a certain place, there are two ways to carry out the work. One way is to help the church in that locality in the carrying out of its work. The other way is to assume full leadership in the church in that locality after the church has handed itself over to us. Since we are all before the Lord, we must be honest about our situation. Now all of you are willing to let me take the lead; I wish to know from you what kind of leadership you are expecting from me. In other words, do you want me to come here just to help you, or do you want me to assume full leadership?"

I remember very clearly that after I said this the leading elder stood up to say that, as the representative of the elders, he would like to hand the church entirely to me and would ask me to assume full leadership. After a while, a senior co-worker also stood up to say that, as the representative of the co-workers, he would like to hand over the work and would ask me to assume full leadership. Following that, the deacons, represented by one of the brothers, also indicated to me that they were willing to put themselves fully under my leadership. Therefore, I said, "Thank the Lord that all of you co-workers, elders, and deacons have expressed the same desire. Therefore, I accept."

At that time I told them, "First, I hope that there would not be any change in personnel in both the work and the service in the church. The elders will still be elders, the co-workers will still be co-workers, and the deacons will remain as deacons. The former practices, however, must all be stopped tonight and should exist no more. Starting tomorrow morning, all of the practices must be new. The first thing to be done is to set up the deacons' office for the deacons to serve there. Everything is to be done in a new way; the old way definitely must not be used." Then I asked two sisters to be in the deacons' office to establish principles for all the services. Due to the limitation in time, I intended to gradually rearrange the services of the elders and of the deacons, as well as the work of the co-workers.

Later two things happened. First, the senior co-worker who had represented all the co-workers in handing themselves over actually had not really handed himself over. Shortly after he did this, the two sisters that I had designated to be in charge of the deacons' office told me that whenever I returned to Taiwan, that brother would come in to tell them to do differently from whatever I had arranged. I told them, "It does not matter. While I am here, just do according to what I have arranged. When I am gone, if that brother does not want it, then just forget it." Therefore, there was a problem that occurred in 1961 in the church in Manila which did not happen suddenly. Instead, the cause had been hidden there from the very beginning.

Second, when I arrived in the Philippines in the spring of 1954, the elders came to meet with me. At that time one of the leading brothers said he realized that under my leadership the elders could no longer be elders in name only but had to give all of their strength and time. He felt that he could not give himself fully and that he also did not have the adequate time. Therefore, in the presence of everyone he wanted to resign his eldership. His word was very honest and very sincere. All of the other elders followed him, wanting to resign from the eldership. At this time the dissenting senior co-worker said that he too wanted to resign from the eldership and asked me to appoint some new elders. So I responded by saying that I needed to pray and seek the leading of the Lord and that before I appointed new elders, the original elders must continue their responsibilities.

After four weeks had passed, they urged me again and again to appoint the elders quickly. However, the more they urged me, the more I felt that I needed to slow down. During this period of seeking and waiting, I continually contacted the older saints, especially the serving sisters and the co-workers, inquiring about their feelings. They gave me their feelings as to which elders ought to remain in the eldership and which brothers should also be added as elders.

One afternoon, that dissenting senior co-worker came to the place where I lived and came directly into my room to urge me to get the matter of the eldership resolved. At that time, I sensed that he really did not want to give up his eldership but was merely trying to retreat in order to advance. He was trying to do this because in the past the elders had not always listened to him. He wanted me to make a new arrangement in the hope that I would openly declare him to be the number one elder. Then others would have to listen to him in the future. Because I had such a sense in my spirit, I immediately told him in all frankness not to try to use me. Then I went back to pray. I inwardly sensed the Lord telling me not to be maneuvered by others but to make the new and proper arrangements according to my real sense derived through the fellowship with all of the saints.

After another week, the elders invited me to be with them, asking me what final decisions I had made. I then fellow-shipped with them my feeling, saying, "Of all the elders, only two will remain whereas another four new ones will be added." The ones retained did not include that senior co-worker; the ones added also did not include him. At that time whether they agreed or not, they had to comply because they had begged me to make the arrangements.

After the transfer of the eldership, something immediately happened to test the newly established elders. At that time there was a certain brother who was coming to Manila. Due to his relationship with the church in Manila in the early days, the brothers wondered whether they ought to invite him to preach the gospel. The two original elders did not necessarily agree with inviting him, but since they did not wish to offend him, they wanted to act in a diplomatic way. The four newly added elders, being serious in their undertaking, definitely did not agree. Unable to settle the issue among themselves, they came to ask me. I told them that I was not an elder in the church in Manila. The church in Manila had been given to the service of the six of them, so they should pray earnestly to see how things should be handled. This was their business; they had to make the decision before the Lord.

The original elders said that since this brother was a pop-ular evangelist and the church in Manila needed to preach the gospel, it would be all right to invite him just to do the work of preaching the gospel. The new elders said that since this brother was not taking the same path as we were but was a traveling evangelist, it would not be proper to invite him to carry out his ministry. They also said that though the church needed to preach the gospel, the church more urgently needed the building up. For the building up of the church it would not be absolutely necessary to invite this brother to preach the gospel. Moreover, they felt that since the church in Manila had already been handed over to me to be built up under my leadership, they should set aside this matter for the time being. Since the original elders felt that they did not have a more convincing or stronger argument, they finally agreed not to invite this brother.

WE BEING RESPONSIBLE TO PLANT AND WATER, BUT GOD CAUSING THE GROWTH

The purpose of going over this history is so that we would realize that the turmoil in the church in Manila in 1961 did not begin in 1961. Rather, the seed was planted there in the beginning. I visited the Philippines yearly for eleven years. Aside from Manila I did not go anywhere else; I worked only in Manila. Within me I knew where the element of rejection lay, but I did not reveal it. My attitude was that as long as the church in Manila did not openly reject me, I would just do the work of sowing, planting, and watering. I did not care for what existed in Manila; I only sowed, planted, and watered. Each time I came, I would not touch anything negative but would sow, plant, and water in a positive way. I was very clear within that one day this place would reject me, but until that day came, I had to take the opportunity to sow, plant, and water. It was not until the real rejection became open and manifest that I stopped coming to Manila. However, I was still waiting to see if what I had sown, planted, and watered would bring forth some fruit.

In 1961 turmoil arose, and the church in Manila truly and completely rejected me. The opposing ones wrote on a long bench in the old meeting hall: "Down with the four elders; cast out Witness Lee." When the news reached me, I thought, "Will there be any result of my sowing, planting, and watering here for the past eleven years?" On the following morning, an elder who customarily attended morning watch at the old meeting hall saw four guards guarding the meeting hall and a notice posted on the door declaring that no one without the express permission of the Board of Trustees could enter the meeting hall. The elders telegraphed me that very day to tell me about the real situation and asked me what should be done since the meeting hall had been taken over. I did not know how to reply. After looking to the Lord for more than a day, I sent a reply telegram saying that they should negotiate with the two main opposing ones. Subsequently, however, the brothers found another hall in which to meet.

Today I am very happy and at ease because I can see that the work of sowing, planting, and watering during those eleven years has yielded fruit. At that time, some of the brothers were still small "tree seedlings"—only sprouts with hardly any growth. Today those brothers have become elders. Some who were not attractive then have become quite beautiful now. There is a brother who is now an elder. It was difficult at that time to discern whether he was a little "plant" or a "piece of stone." Now he has grown to be a very sturdy "tree," full of the organic function. When I listen to his prayers or pay attention to his sharing, I feel that he is inwardly bright with clear revelation. The sky above him is clear. Thank and praise the Lord. This work is not of man but of God; it is God who causes such ones to grow.

This kind of open fellowship is especially for the young saints to see that we should not do the work of an organization. We should only do the organic work of a living organism. The reason we are happy is because we can see the manifestation of the organic function in this organism. Due to God's mercy and grace, during those eleven years I did not do the work of an organization; rather, bit by bit I was there doing an organic work. Today everyone can see the function of this organism. The church is God's garden in which there are many big trees as well as many smaller ones growing. They will all grow and bear fruit, manifesting the organic function.

More than one hundred churches in the southern islands of the Philippines have been raised up through the sixty lessons of the *Fundamental Truths in the Scriptures*. This was not due to organization or man's arrangement. This was entirely the result of the development of the Lord's organic function within the saints. They also testified that the life-studies have rendered them tremendous help, not just giving them some outward supply or some understanding of objective doctrines, but causing them to grow in life and to have some subjective and real experiences. More than ten years ago when I went to Mindanao, what I saw at that time had already brought me much joy. Today when I see so many of the saints in Mindanao fervently seeking the Lord by reading spiritual literature, I am filled with even greater joy within. Through fellowship I have discovered that they have a clear vision. This is proof that the churches in Mindanao are not the work of an organization but entirely the issue of the life supply in the Body of Christ and the result of the manifestation of the organic function. This deeply touches me within.

PROPAGATING THE TRUTH IN THE LORD'S RECOVERY
THROUGH THE DEVELOPMENT
OF THE ORGANIC FUNCTION

Hence, we see in perspective that the Lord has given the entire Philippines to His recovery because the Lord's pure gospel and His complete truth are in His recovery. The Spaniards brought Catholicism to the Philippines, and later the missionaries from the United States came to work here. Consequently, the Philippines is overall a Christian country. Nevertheless, most Filipinos know only a little about God and have heard only a fraction of the gospel, which in most cases was not the pure gospel. This is beside the fact that most know little concerning the truth. The people here know about the existence of God and also fear God, but there is not much preaching of the pure gospel and even less speaking of the complete truth. Thank the Lord that He gave us a period of eleven years to open up the entire New Testament, chapter by chapter and verse by verse. During those eleven years we studied exhaustively, and what the Lord unveiled to us has now been put into print for you to have in your hands. There are many rich truths within that need to be revealed to God's children.

The New Testament was completed during the apostolic age. However, for two thousand years man's understanding of the New Testament has been incomplete. The Bible that is now in the hands of Christians has not been that open. Today there are many expositions of the Bible in Christianity. Among these expositions there are also many interpretations of the truth. Most of the interpretations, however, stop with the light and revelation of one hundred and fifty years ago, whereas the light and revelation in the life-studies are up-to-date and also complete and rich. For example, the Triune God's dispensing of life and God's New Testament economy are altogether new revelations. This kind of terminology and speaking cannot be found in any publications in Christianity. However, in the Lord's recovery there are many messages of this kind. All these are the latest revelations gradually shown to us by God during the last ten to twenty years. Take the New Jerusalem for example. You cannot find one book in Christianity explaining and developing all the items of life related to the New Jerusalem in such a thorough way as you may read in the publications in the Lord's recovery.

The gospel that we preach in the Lord's recovery is the purest, highest, and most complete gospel. For example, concerning the Lord's death on the cross, where in any other book can you find that the Lord had seven statuses when He suffered death on the cross? This proves that the light which the Lord has given us is clear and complete. Christianity in the Philippines has a history of at least three hundred years. There may be almost fifty million Christians in the Philippines, but they are all in an unclear state—they are in a cloud. People know there is a God and have heard a bit of the gospel, but the sky over them is not clear but cloudy. They seem to know God, but in reality they do not know God. They are altogether ignorant of what God is all about, what He is doing, and what He wants to gain today. Therefore, we must receive the burden to preach to them the divine truths in the Lord's recovery.

No one is able to destroy or overthrow the Lord's recovery on this earth because it has a very solid foundation. The Lord's recovery, as God's garden flourishing abundantly, is firmly rooted. Recently several hundred young people have come into the church life. We know this is just the beginning; thousands more will come into the Lord's recovery to enter into the divine truths. Furthermore, one day they will all be able to stand up before millions to preach the pure gospel and to speak the divine truths. I have the boldness to make such a prediction and also the faith that this word will soon come true.

Hence, we must pay attention to equipping ourselves so that we may be suitable for the Lord's use. In this way, through us the Lord will be able to gain our locality, as well as the whole earth, with the pure gospel, the complete truth, and the normal and proper church life.

First we must be clear that the Lord's move is definitely not organizational but organic. We have seen through history that from 1950, when the Lord began His work in Manila, to the present, we have not been doing an organizational work but one of sowing, planting, and watering so that the church of the living God can develop her organic function. Today in the Philippines, all of the fruit has come not through organization but through the organic growth of the church producing that which is living and of life to become an organic Body. In the Lord's recovery we do not emphasize organization, nor do we pay attention to position and reputation. The grace that we have received is the grace of life; this life is Christ Himself, who today is the all-inclusive Spirit, the Triune God experienced by us. He is growing in us and in the church. The more He grows, the more He multiplies, and the more He flourishes. Through the church as the organic Body and God's garden, the Lord will be able to fulfill His purpose and accomplish His economy.

CHAPTER THREE

LEARNING AND EXPLAINING
THE TRUTH

What delights us beyond all else in the church is seeing so many young people being raised up. When we see the older people, we also cannot help but smile, because they are the fathers, the base of the church. Without the older ones, there would be no young people. However, when we see the young ones, our hearts leap for joy because they are the future of the church. Therefore, when the young people rise up to serve, our joy is magnified. Nevertheless, those who serve practically in the churches in every place, especially the young ones, must learn some skills and secrets. Since you have a heart to serve, you must learn how to lead the saints. If you do not know how to lead others, how can you serve? If you do not have any ability, how then can you lead? Therefore, I hope that we would all learn some solid lessons in the matter of service.

THE WHOLE EARTH
NEEDING THE GOSPEL AND THE TRUTH

Paul said that he was sent not only to preach the gospel but also to teach the truth (1 Tim. 2:7; 2 Tim. 1:11). This indicates that it is not sufficient just to preach the gospel; we should also teach the truth. The main emphasis of the Bible is the gospel and the truth. The gospel is God Himself, and the truth is also God Himself. We must study the Bible thoroughly until we can see that the gospel is God Himself and that the truth is also God Himself. The gospel is not merely a kind of message but God Himself; the truth is not merely a doctrine but God Himself.

We must have the realization that what the whole earth needs today is the gospel and the truth. The Bible was completed two thousand years ago and was given to the church. Unfortunately, due to the degradation of the church, the light of the gospel dissipated and the light of the truth also became dim. From the history of the church, we see that after the apostles passed away, the light of the gospel and of the truth gradually faded until the seventh century when it was totally lost for a duration of ten centuries. World history calls this period the Dark Ages. Then came the time of the Reformation when the primary work of the reformers was to release the truths in the Bible. From then on the light of the truth began to rise like the sun from the east at daybreak. Slowly the long night passed away and a ray of morning sun began to appear. Although the light at that time was weak, it shone more and more. Today it can be said that the light of the gospel and of the truth is shining as bright and full as the sun at noonday.

However, much of the light of the gospel and of the truth has been released only within the Lord's recovery. Outside of the publications in the Lord's recovery, the most recent light one can find is light that was released in the middle of the nineteenth century. We may say that the light in Christian publications has been extremely sparse for the past one and a half centuries. As a result, the theology taught today in every country covers the light of the truth only up to one hundred fifty years ago. In the Lord's recovery, however, the light of the truth is up-to-date.

Three hundred years ago the Philippines was under the occupation of the Spaniards. Spain was a Catholic country. Even though five centuries ago the Reformation brought in the light of the truth, it did not have much impact on the basic nature of Catholicism. Therefore, when the Spaniards came to the Philippines, instead of bringing the truths recovered through the Reformation, they brought the old Catholic theology of the Dark Ages. Through their political power they spread Catholicism to all of the Philippines.

Thirty years ago when I first came to the Philippines, I spent some time observing the situation in Catholicism. I went to the so-called "Cathedral of Jesus the Black Nazarene." There was a sculpture of this so-called "Jesus the Black Nazarene," the toes of which had been worn down from being touched by the Catholics. When I saw this, I could not help but shake my head and sigh, thinking to myself, "O pitiful ones, how could you be deceived to such an extent?" I really hated that superstitious situation. One day I saw many people crying and yelling in the streets, so I asked the brothers what was happening. They told me, "These people are repenting for having robbed and stolen from others. However, after repenting today, tomorrow they will rob and steal again." I was really grieved in my heart because that situation was absolutely contrary to the gospel and the truth.

Not only is the Philippines like this, but Catholicism in South America is also in the same condition. I have lived in the United States for over twenty years, and by observing the situation I have discovered that the Americans are equally superstitious. This fully proves that what the whole earth needs today is the light of the gospel and the light of the truth. Regardless of nationality or race, people need the pure and high gospel and truth.

THE LORD'S RECOVERY BEING
THE RECOVERY OF THE LIGHT OF THE TRUTH

The Lord's recovery is the recovery of the light of the truth. In the past sixty years the Lord has been opening up the Bible to us day by day, chapter by chapter, and verse by verse. He will continue to do so until all of the truths from Genesis to Revelation are completely transparent, opened, and unveiled to us. We may say that until now there has not been another group of Christians who has spoken on Genesis chapter two and especially on the tree of life as clearly as they have been spoken in the Lord's recovery. In the same way, today there is no one outside of the Lord's recovery who can speak on the truth in the last two chapters of Revelation regarding the New Jerusalem to the degree of clarity that we have seen and spoken it.

In 1963 I was invited to work in America in eastern Texas. One night after I returned home to my hospitality, I saw a young man, a Southern Baptist believer, who was dedicated to gospel preaching. He was sitting in the study making a telephone call, inviting his friend to come to the meetings. He told the friend that he was attending a preaching meeting with a very unusual message and that he hoped that he would by all means fly over to attend. When I heard this, I shook my head, thinking he was crazy. What surprised me was that on the next evening his friend came from West Texas. That night I spoke on the relationship between the first two chapters of Genesis and the last two chapters of Revelation. After listening, this one was captured by the Lord and confessed that he had never heard this kind of message before. He also stated that he would definitely receive the teaching and take this way. As the next day was the Lord's Day, he had to preach a sermon so he went back to West Texas to fulfill his duty. The following Monday morning he brought his wife. After she heard one message, she also expressed a desire to take this way.

This example shows you that even such an advanced Christian country as America is short of biblical truth. Therefore, the most urgent need on this earth today is the truth of this age. The Lord has placed the responsibility of spreading the truth upon our shoulders. Although we do not have a large number of serving ones, we should each pick up this burden to learn the truth, to preach it everywhere, and to bring ten others into the knowledge of the truth and perfect them to do what we are doing. If we do this, then in three to five years there will be a tremendous multiplication and increase among us. In the Philippines if there were forty thousand who knew the truth and could also explain it to others, then they would be able to spread the truth to the entire country. That would be a glorious sight.

Approximately thirty years ago when the Philippines first came out from under more than forty years of rule by the United States, the English language was still not very common. Now the situation is no longer the same; we see English being taught even in the elementary schools in Mindanao. I truly believe that one day not only the light of the gospel but also the light of the truth in the Lord's recovery will be spread to all of the Philippines, just like the English language. Even the young ones who are newly saved will be able to utter the truths readily.

What we call the light of the truth is actually the light of the gospel. The so-called gospel that most Christians preach is too shallow and too low. The gospel actually includes all of the truths in the Bible. Today the Bible is published and widely propagated all over the world. Many people have the Bible, but to them it is neither open nor easily understood. When they read it, they use their mind to comprehend it, so there is no way for them to see the spiritual mysteries. Consider Ephesians 5 for example. When people—whether Christians or unbelievers—read this chapter they all feel good about it because they consider it a chapter on husbands loving their wives and wives submitting to their husbands (vv. 25, 22). In reality all wives want their husbands to love them and also wish to submit to their husbands. The wives already have these concepts in them; there is no need to read the Bible in order to have such an understanding. Similarly all husbands desire to love their wives, but their greatest problem is that their wives are not submissive. Without being taught by the Bible, the husbands already have these concepts within them.

However, Ephesians 5 not only speaks about these two things, it also reveals a much deeper truth, which is that we must be filled with God in spirit (v. 18). Yet when people read this verse, nearly all of them have their eyes veiled. They do not know what it is to be in spirit and what the spirit is. They also do not know who God is and how God can fill them. This is the kind of understanding that people, including Christians, have of the Bible. They know the superficial word of the Bible, but almost no one apprehends its hidden truths and mysteries.

Most Christians when reading the Bible only see that it teaches people to be forbearing, patient, kind, righteous, and temperate. They consider this kind of teaching to be good and proper and more or less the same as the teachings of the Chinese Confucianists. They are totally ignorant of the revelation in the Bible regarding God's economy and God's mysteries. To most people, including the common Christian, the Bible is a closed book. Consider the Gospel of Matthew. Almost no one understands why Matthew chapter one records Christ's genealogy or why it is presented in the way that it is. Thank the Lord that today in the Lord's recovery the Bible is no longer a closed book. If we would read the Bible along with the life-study messages, we would be able to see the significance of every name. The more we read, the more we will be clear and the more we will have the sense that the entire book has been opened to us. As a result, we will be able to enter into the depths of Matthew and come to the knowledge of the true significance of the divine revelation.

For this reason, I have been encouraging all the saints in America and in Taiwan to spend two hours a day to study the Bible with the help of the life-study messages. In this way, the entire New Testament can be read through in four years. I hope that all of the young people will spend the time. Then in four years you will become excellent Bible teachers, able to present the New Testament clearly and logically and to meet the Lord's great need in every place.

SPENDING TIME TO ENTER INTO THE TRUTHS IN THE LORD'S RECOVERY

A young person who is sloppy at age fifteen will be a foolish person at age eighteen. However, if he is willing to study hard during high school, he can learn many things. If he continues with another four years of college, by age twenty-two he will be more enlightened inwardly and able to teach others. The difference between those who are learned and those who are unlearned is very great. Today those who have a college education are distinguished in society. Thus, even if you are no longer a young person, it would be best for you to go back to school to get a college education if possible. Otherwise, it will be difficult to convince others.

We are certainly happy to see the elderly saints, but it is very difficult for us to demand that they spend more effort to pursue the truth. They love the Lord and also His word. They know Genesis 1:26, realizing that God created man in His own image. They understand Ephesians 1:4, knowing that God chose us in Christ. They are clear about Proverbs 9:10, recognizing that the fear of Jehovah is the beginning of wisdom and that the knowledge of the Holy One is understanding. They are able to testify to others, saying, "The Bible is very good; it tells us that God created us in His image, that He chose us in Christ, and that today He has become our wisdom." This is more than sufficient. We cannot ask for more. However, if the young people among us were to study the Word in the same way, this would be very disappointing. Why should an eighteen year old study the Word like a sixty-eight year old? That way of studying is not bad, but only for an elderly saint. An eighteen year old must study the Bible utilizing a more in-depth method, just as Solomon said that we should remember our Lord in the days of our youth (Eccl. 12:1). The young people must learn the highest truths while they are in their youth.

Concerning God's Creation

First, the Bible reveals God's creation (Gen. 1—2). In God's creation there are two important points—one is the creation of life, and the other is the creation of man. The creation of life is the most unusual aspect of God's creation. People today promote the building up of their countries, but no matter how much building work they do, they can never produce life. At best they can build some robots that resemble man but do not have man's life within. Regardless of how far technology has advanced in producing more and more sophisticated computers, it still does not have the ability to create a living brain. Only God can create life. Genesis chapter one shows us that God firstly created the inanimate objects and then the living things. When He created the living things, God started from the lowest form of life and then progressed to the higher forms of life. This is the process of God's creation of life.

The highest form of the created life is the human life. Human life is the highest life among the lives created by God. This life is one that resembles the life of God; it is a life created according to God's image. God's image is love, light, holiness, and righteousness. Since the human life has God's image, it also has love, light, holiness and righteousness, making it the highest created life. Of course, in the universe there is still a higher life—the life of God. In the entire universe the highest life is God's life. Therefore, in Genesis chapter two the tree of life depicts God's life. Man was placed before the tree of life, indicating that God wanted man to take Him as the highest life so that man would live out God's life in the human life. This is the truth concerning God's creation.

Concerning Man's Fall

Second, the Bible speaks about the fall of man, which is recorded in Genesis chapter three. There are also two important points concerning the fall of man. First, when man fell, there was a charge of sin against him before God, and man became a sinner condemned by God. Second, man now had the sinful nature within him as the result of Satan's coming into man's flesh. Satan tempted man to eat the fruit of the tree of the knowledge of good and evil. This fruit denotes Satan, just as the fruit of the tree of life denotes God. If man had eaten of the tree of life, he would have gained God. However, man ate the fruit of the tree of the knowledge of good and evil, receiving Satan into his flesh, issuing in the sinful nature being in man's flesh. This sinful nature is called *sin* in the Bible. Therefore, when man fell, not only was there a charge of sin against him before God, but also the sinful nature was in his flesh.

Concerning God's Incarnation

The third great truth in the Bible is God's becoming flesh. There are three main points concerning God's incarnation: the bringing of God into man, the accomplishment of redemption, and the termination of the old creation.

First, God became flesh to bring God into man. Although God created man in His image, He did not put Himself into man at that time. It was not until the incarnation that God brought Himself into man. Therefore, Jesus the Nazarene, who was conceived in and brought forth through Mary, was a God-man. Outwardly He was a man, but inwardly He was God. Outwardly, as a man He had the human nature; inwardly, as God He had the divine nature. He was a God-man with the human nature as well as the divine nature. His divine nature lived in His human nature, and His human nature expressed His divine nature. In His human nature were all kinds of human virtues, the principal ones being love, light, holiness, and righteousness. In the record of the four Gospels in the New Testament we see the Lord Jesus, who was God yet man, being full of love, light, holiness, and righteousness. In His human virtues of love, light, holiness, and righteousness were the divine attributes. In other words, the divine attributes in the humanity of the Lord Jesus strengthened, enriched, and uplifted His human virtues so that the love, light, holiness, and righteousness that He lived out were the most outstanding, excellent, and highest virtues.

Normally when we preach the gospel, we feel like we do not have much to say. We are able to say that it is good to believe in Jesus, but we are unable to explain why. Most Christians can only tell others that believing in Jesus is a good thing because it will save them from going to hell and will give them peace and prosperity. Some unbelievers after hearing this might say, "You believers are superstitious. You only talk about hell, prosperity, and peace. What is the difference between this and worshipping Buddha?" I hope that from now on when we see our friends and relatives, we would say to them, "Let me tell you who Jesus was. He was a God-man, having both the human nature and the divine nature. His divine nature lived in His human nature, and His human nature expressed His divine nature. In His human nature there were human virtues—love, light, holiness and righteousness—which were strengthened, enriched, and uplifted by His divine attributes. Therefore, the virtues of love, light, holiness, and righteousness that He lived out were excellent."

You may ask how those who have never heard the gospel will be able to understand all of this. Actually, you ask this because you underestimate them. If we can understand, they can also understand. They are the same as we are; there is hardly any difference between us. Therefore, what we can understand, they definitely can also understand. An American brother testified that for a period of time he used the diagram of the three circles, which depicts the spirit, soul, and body, and spoke about man's three parts as his unique topic in gospel preaching. The result was that after contacting over five hundred people during a period of several years, over three hundred were saved. Today many Christians, even many pastors and preachers, do not necessarily understand the truth conveyed in the diagram of the three circles. Nevertheless, we must have the faith within that as long as we speak, those who listen will definitely be saved. Do not worry that people will not be able to understand.

From now on we must stop preaching the superficial gospel, telling people that believing in Jesus is good because the sick will be healed and the poor will become rich. This is not the gospel; this is superstition and is altogether deceiving. Today some people practice divine healing, but in the end they are cheating people. Strictly speaking, divine healing is a power of the age to come (Heb. 6:5). We should not preach this; instead, we should use the diagram of the three circles to preach on the three parts of man. When I spoke on the three circles twenty years ago, a brother who was a traveling preacher from the Brethren assembly and who had established Brethren meetings in more than ten places was greatly touched, because he had never heard this kind of speaking before. Later, not only did he learn about the three circles, but wherever he went, he also spoke this truth. I hope that all of us would also learn the truths diligently and speak them everywhere.

The second main point of God's incarnation is that this God-man went to the cross to suffer death to accomplish eternal redemption. The third main point is that He terminated, or put to an end, all the things of the old creation on the cross.

Group b sharing Concerning God's Dispensing

The fourth great truth in the Bible is God's dispensing. The noun form of *dispensing* is *dispensation*. Unfortunately, this word has been spoiled by the theology taught in Christianity. Whenever this word is mentioned, theologians understand it as the different methods by which God deals with people. Every dispensation is a way that God deals with His people. When it came time for the Chinese theologians to

translate this term, they had difficulty and could only translate it as *age*, indicating that God deals with people
differently in various ages. In reality, this term in Latin and
English theology denotes God's arrangement, which is the
divine administration. However, when we use this term today,
we are referring not to God's arrangement or administration
but to God's dispensing. Therefore, for the sake of differentia-
tion, we do not use *dispensation,* but rather *dispensing.*

In God's plan He not only became flesh, but He also dispenses Himself into His chosen people. How does God dispense
Himself into man? First we must see that the death of the
Lord Jesus was not just a termination. The Lord died but was
also resurrected. His resurrection was a new beginning. His
death was the termination of everything in the old creation,
but He did not stop there. After everything was terminated,
there was a new beginning—resurrection. Peter tells us that
through Christ's resurrection we were all regenerated (1 Pet.
1:3). Paul said that through His resurrection the Lord Jesus
as the last Adam became a life-giving Spirit (1 Cor. 15:45).
This means that in Christ's resurrection He became a life-
giving Spirit to enter into all those who believe into Him.

The life-giving Spirit enters into us firstly to regenerate
us. Regeneration is God dispensing Himself into us. To be
regenerated is to be born of God. Once we are born of God, we
have God's life in us, which is God Himself. This may be likened to the fact that when a father begets a son, the father
dispenses himself into the son so that the father's life and
nature are in the son. Since the father is human, the son is
also human. In the same way, when God dispenses Himself
into us, we are regenerated with God's life and nature to
become God's children (John 1:12-13; 1 John 5:1).

The life-giving Spirit enters into us secondly to sanctify us
and thirdly to transform us. Sanctification is for us to be separated, and transformation is for us to be changed in nature.
Fourth, God conforms us to Christ's image and fifth, He glori-
fies us so that we may enter into glory. Regeneration,
sanctification, transformation, conformation, and glorification
are the five steps of God's work in dispensing Himself into
us. The church today must daily allow the Lord to do the work

of sanctification, transformation, and conformation. At the end of the age, when the Lord Jesus comes again, He will glorify us, that is, He will come out of us as glory (Phil. 3:21). Then we will enter into His glory. That will be the kingdom age, which will last for one thousand years. Afterward, the New Jerusalem will come as the ultimate expression of God's dispensing. This expression is God and man becoming one entity—God as man's inward life and nature, and man as God's outward expression. This expression is glory, and this glory is the issue of the mingling of God and man—the New Jerusalem as the consummate expression.

PREACHING THE TRUTHS IN THE LORD'S RECOVERY AS THE GOSPEL

These four great points—God's creation, man's fall, God's becoming flesh, and God's dispensing—are the major truths in the Bible, from God's creation to the New Jerusalem, from Genesis to Revelation. Although they are the major truths, they are not difficult to comprehend. They can be easily understood by the young ones as well as by the elderly ones. We must preach these truths as the gospel to others. When we go to preach, whether others can understand or not depends on how we speak. If we speak clearly, plainly, and logically, then everyone will be able to understand. If we speak clumsily and ambiguously, then no one will be able to understand. Therefore, if we have the burden within that the Lord's recovery would spread to every place, it is not enough just to preach the superficial gospel of Christianity. We must announce to people the major truths in the Bible as the gospel. For this reason we must study them diligently.

When we speak to our relatives and friends, we do not need to preach everything all at once but may divide our speaking over several occasions, speaking clearly, little by little, once a week. In general, the educational level among people today has been raised, and people's reasoning and logic skills are more advanced and enriched than in the past. Furthermore, most people have some philosophical ideas and are able to ponder over all kinds of questions related to human life, questions requiring high levels of psychological reasoning. If we only talk about peace and prosperity, people will not be happy because they will not be satisfied. However, if we preach these four great truths, people will be appreciative because these truths will match their inner condition, raising their interest and their thinking concerning human life, as well as providing them the highest answers to the true meaning of human life. If someone is saved as a result of this, his salvation will be a surpassing salvation.

We believe that this is the only way we can bring the Lord back as well as meet the need of human society in its present vain condition. The result of society's civilization and progress has been an unremitting emptiness within man. Only the high truths in the Lord's recovery can fill up this emptiness. Therefore, we should bear this burden to diligently study the truth to the extent that we can expound the truth and announce the truth. This is to truly preach the gospel. This is the preaching of the high gospel. Paul said that God had commissioned him to preach the gospel and to teach the truth (1 Tim. 2:7). In the same way, this commission has been given to us today. I hope that we would all receive this commission to actively preach the gospel and teach the truth.

CHAPTER FOUR

THE FIRST GREAT PILLAR
IN THE LORD'S RECOVERY—THE TRUTH

Scripture Reading: 1 Tim. 2:4, 7; 3:15; 2 Tim. 3:7, 15-16

THE LORD'S RECOVERY
BEING THE RECOVERY OF THE TRUTH

Today the whole earth needs the truth of the Lord that is in His Word. Regrettably, however, the Bible, the divine Word, has not been fully opened to the world. Thus, it has not been possible for people to fully know the truth of the Lord. At the most, Christians are able to boast that the holy Word of God has been published into many languages and propagated over the whole earth. Yet they are not able to say that after reading the Bible, regardless of which language, they have been able to truly understand the deep mysteries within it. They have been able to understand the superficial meanings of the things revealed in the Bible according to their own culture, philosophy, tradition, customs, ethics, living, and morality but have had no way of comprehending the mysteries of the truths in it. The mysteries of the truths in the Bible are very deep and profound. We need the spiritual enlightening of the Spirit of God to understand them, and we also need to spend time to dig them out (cf. 1 Cor. 2:10-14).

The truths in the holy Word of the Lord were completed approximately two thousand years ago, but over a period of a little more than one thousand years they seemed to slowly vanish. Only in the last few centuries have the truths again been released little by little through the zealous and careful study of many lovers of the Lord. This is what we refer to as the Lord's recovery. The Lord's recovery is the recovery of all the truths in the Bible that were lost. Thus, the recovery of the truth is one of the great pillars in the Lord's recovery. The Lord's recovery lies with the recovery of the knowledge of the truth.

HAVING THE FULL KNOWLEDGE OF THE TRUTH FOR THE SPREAD OF THE LORD'S RECOVERY

The New Testament says repeatedly that we should know the truth. Moreover, when referring to this matter, Paul repeatedly says that we should come to the full knowledge of the truth (1 Tim. 2:4; 2 Tim. 2:25; 3:7; Titus 1:1). This means that we must know not just a small part or one aspect of the truth but rather the truth in its entirety and in all of its aspects. Paul also said that the church is the pillar and base of the truth (1 Tim. 3:15). This implies that the truth in the Bible is like a large building that is not one-sided but complete on all sides with a foundation and a roof. If we are going to spread the Lord's recovery today, we must know the truth and be able to expound the truth. For this reason, we must know every side of the truth without any biases or particular leanings.

The truth not only has many sides but also includes many crucial items. For example, the Bible speaks about God, Christ, the Holy Spirit, the believers, the church, the kingdom, and the New Jerusalem. The Bible begins with God, then continues with God's creation, man's fall, God's redemption, and God's entering into man to be man's life for man to be regenerated, sanctified, renewed, transformed, conformed into His own image, and ultimately to be brought fully into glory. In the midst of all these matters, the Bible also shows us the believers and the corporate church. This corporate church brings in the kingdom, consummating in the ultimate expression, which is the New Jerusalem in the new heaven and new earth. All of these aspects are included in the truths of the Bible.

Considering the deeper and more detailed truths, the Bible speaks about the two aspects of God's complete salvation of us: redemption and salvation. The aspect of redemption includes forgiveness, cleansing, justification, reconciliation, and acceptance; the aspect of salvation includes His coming to regenerate, sanctify, renew, and transform us, so as to conform us to His image and ultimately to bring us into His glory. This is God's complete salvation. We must diligently learn all of these things, obtain the knowledge of them, and be able to speak them clearly to others.

LEARNING TO KNOW THE MYSTERIES OF THE TRUTH

The above points merely show the different aspects of the truth, not the mysteries of the truth in their entirety. What are the mysteries of the truth in the Bible? What is the central mystery of the Bible? In brief, in the holy Word of God there is a central mystery. This central mystery is that the Triune God wants to dispense Himself into man. Our God is the Triune God, and He wants to dispense Himself into His chosen ones to be their life and everything. This is the kernel, the core, of the mystery in the Bible.

God Creating Man in His Image
for the Purpose of Dispensing Himself into Man

Unfortunately, many Bible readers do not and cannot see this point. For example, when they read Genesis chapter one, all they can see is that God created the heavens and the earth, that He then created all the living things, and that He finally created man. However, they do not see that the purpose of God's creation of man was to make it possible for Him to dispense Himself into man. They may realize from their reading that God created man according to His image, but they do not understand at all why God created man according to His image.

God created man in His own image so that He would be able to put Himself into man. Romans chapter nine says that God made man to be a vessel (v. 23). A vessel is a container made to hold something. For example, to hold a round object, a vessel for round objects must be made; to hold a square object, a vessel made for square objects must be made. A vessel is made in the shape of the object it is to contain. The hand has five fingers; thus, for a glove to be worn by the hand, it must resemble the five fingers of the hand. When a glove is

Tom

Therefore, after many years I still did not know the meaning of eating the Lord. Then one day I read where Paul tells Timothy, "The Lord be with your spirit" (2 Tim. 4:22). At first I did not understand what it was for the Lord to be with my spirit. First, I wondered how the Lord could be with my spirit since He is in the heavens. Second, I really did not understand what my spirit was. I knew that in my body there was a stomach and intestines and that in my head there was a brain, but I did not know what my spirit was. I really did not understand. Subsequently I read that the Lord had said, "The words which I have spoken to you are spirit and are life" (John 6:63). Again I did not understand how words could become spirit. Then I read John chapter three where the Lord told Nicodemus, "Unless one is born anew, he cannot see the kingdom of God." Nicodemus thought that to be born anew was to return to the mother's womb, so he said, "How can a man be born when he is old? He cannot enter a second time into his mother's womb and be born, can he?" The Lord answered that to be born anew is to be born of water and of the Spirit because that which is born of the Spirit is spirit (vv. 3-6). The more I read, the more I became puzzled. When the Spirit entered into my spirit, I was regenerated. Then, where was my spirit? What was my spirit? After reading those verses, I was absolutely confused and without a clue as to what they referred to.

The Mystery of the Divine Trinity

After many years I gradually began to see the clear light and was able to thoroughly understand the revelation, realizing that God Himself is Spirit (4:24). Our God is triune; He is the Father, the Son, and the Spirit. However, the Father, Son, and Spirit are not three different Gods but one God. One day this God became flesh and came to the earth as a man. It was not just the Son who came, but the Son came with the Father and the Spirit. Therefore, in incarnation, it was not just the Son who came, but the Father, Son, and Spirit all came together.

Most Christians have the concept that when the Son came, He came alone, leaving the Father in the heavens. However, the Gospel of John says clearly that the Son came with the Father. John tells us that while the Lord was on the earth for over thirty years, He was never lonely because the Father was always with Him (8:29; 16:32). Not only so, John also says that the Son was in the Father and that the Father was in the Son (14:10-11). The Father's being with the Son is easy to understand and describe. For example, when the Son went to Galilee, the Father went with Him; when the Son went to Jerusalem, the Father went with Him; and when the Son went to the cross, the Father was also there with Him. This is very easy to describe. However, it is impossible to describe the Son's being in the Father and the Father's being in the Son. The coinhering of the two is truly a mystery.

In John 14:8 Philip came forward and said, "Lord, show us the Father and it is sufficient for us." The disciples had been with the Lord, beholding Him for three and a half years. They had often heard Him speak about the Father yet had never seen Him reveal the Father to them. They thought that if the Lord would simply show them the Father, they would be satisfied. This is similar to the way we believe into the Lord. We also feel that if the Father were to come to us, we would definitely rejoice. However, the Lord was amazed by Philip's question, saying, "Have I been so long a time with you, and you have not known Me, Philip? He who has seen Me has seen the Father; how is it that you say, Show us the Father? Do you not believe that I am in the Father and the Father is in Me?" (vv. 9-10). This statement indicates that the Son and the Father are one. Therefore, when a person sees the Son, he sees the Father. Not only so, the Son is in the Father, and the Father is in the Son.

Following this, the Lord said, "And I will ask the Father, and He will give you another Comforter" (v. 16). Then He also said that the Comforter is "the Spirit of reality, who proceeds from the Father" (15:26). The word *from* in Greek has the sense of *from with*. In other words, the Comforter does not come alone but comes with the Father. Moreover, since the Father is in the Son, the Son also comes. The result is that when the Spirit comes, the Father, Son, and Spirit all come. This is the Triune God.

Most Christians think that the Father is in the heavens and that when the Son resurrected and ascended, He also went to the heavens, sat down at the Father's right hand, and then sent the Spirit down upon the believers so that they could prophesy and speak in tongues. However, the Gospel of John clearly says that the Son is joined to the Father; that the Son sends the Spirit from the Father; that the Spirit does not come alone but comes from the Father and with the Father; and that since the Father is joined to the Son, the Spirit also comes with the Son. When a sinner repents on earth and prays to the Lord, calling on His name, immediately the Spirit comes, bringing the Father with the Son. It is impossible to thoroughly explain such a mystery.

The Story of the Triune God's Entering into Man

When God incarnated, the Son came with the Father and the Spirit. In addition, the Son died on the cross and on the third day resurrected. When He resurrected, Paul says that He became the life-giving Spirit (1 Cor. 15:45). Just as His resurrection is a mystery, so His becoming the life-giving Spirit is also a mystery. Although we cannot comprehend this, it is a fact. As the life-giving Spirit, He is omnipresent—He is both in the heavens and on the earth. This life-giving Spirit is God Himself—the Father, the Son, and the Spirit. When this Spirit comes to us, it is the Triune God coming to us. When this Spirit enters into us, it is the Triune God entering into our spirit. When we confess our sins, repent, and call on the name of the Lord, we sense that something changes inwardly. This change is the entering in of the Spirit. Once the Spirit enters, we feel bright and fresh within. Our spirit is revived, enlivened, and strengthened.

For this reason when we repent, confess our sins, and believe into the Lord Jesus, immediately we sense an inward joy and are completely changed. Formerly there was darkness within us, but once we called on the name of the Lord Jesus, immediately there was light. Formerly we felt oppressed within, but once we called on the Lord, we were liberated. Formerly we were evil to the uttermost, being hateful and full of complaints. We may have even thrown dishes, hit the table, and kicked the chairs. However, once we believed in the Lord Jesus, calling on His name, immediately we felt that the people and things around us all changed and became quite lovable. We also became the most happy people. Why is this? There is no other reason except that the Spirit entered into us. This Spirit is God, the Creator, and our Redeemer, who shed His blood and died on the cross for us. When we pray and call, "Abba Father," we feel sweet within. Who is this "Abba Father"? He is the Spirit. Who is this Spirit? He is the Triune God. This is the mystery of the Triune God in us.

Being Filled Inwardly and Outwardly with the Spirit

In this way the Triune God dispenses Himself into us and also lives in us. Therefore, daily we must breathe Him and pray to Him. Our prayer is just like our breathing. Daily we must also exercise our spirit to receive Him, to eat Him. To eat Him is to receive Him. When we pray and read the Word, we are breathing the spiritual air and eating the spiritual food. Both the spiritual air and the spiritual food are the Spirit. Thus, the result is that we are filled with the Spirit. When we are filled to the extent that we overflow with joy, we will say, "It is no longer I, but it is Christ!" (Gal. 2:20).

It is amazing that we are filled inwardly with the Spirit, yet we would say that the One who lives in us is Christ. This proves that Christ is the Spirit within us. "It is no longer I, but it is Christ who lives in me." This is what many of us have experienced. Consequently, we are inwardly filled with joy, satisfaction, light, and zeal to such an extent that we even are beside ourselves and become "crazy," telling whomever we meet about the Christ in us. By this speaking, the gospel goes out. When we are beside ourselves, we do not care about east or west or heaven or earth, and we are neither shy nor fearful. Wherever we go, we speak to others about Jesus, telling them that Jesus is the most wonderful One. Why is this? This is because we are not only filled with the Spirit within but also have the outpouring of the Spirit upon us. Hence, once we open our mouths, others will be moved because we have the Spirit inwardly and outwardly.

Nevertheless, this is not to say that we have two Spirits, one inside and one outside. We have only one Spirit. The Spirit within us is the essential Spirit whereas the Spirit outside of us is the economical Spirit. The essential Spirit within us makes us joyful, crazy, zealous, and fearless; the economical Spirit outside of us supplies us with authority as we preach, causing our listeners to be subdued so that they must believe. Since we are filled with the essential Spirit inwardly and with the economical Spirit outwardly, we are completely mingled with the Triune God in spirit. God is Spirit, and this Spirit is the Father, the Son, and the Spirit. In other words, this Spirit is the Triune God—the Father, Son, and Spirit—completely filling us and enveloping us. The Spirit who fills us inwardly, the essential Spirit, is like living water for us to drink (John 7:37-39; 1 Cor. 12:13). The Spirit who fills us outwardly, the economical Spirit, is like a mantle of power for us to put on (Luke 24:49; 2 Kings 2:9, 13-15).

The essential Spirit is for our living and enjoyment. When we call on the name of the Lord and enjoy Him, He fills us as the essential Spirit. Then we become ecstatic, burning, and bold, feeling that Jesus is the best. We do not desire anything else but the Lord Jesus. Then when we speak with boldness, proclaiming the name of the Lord, the economical Spirit is poured upon us, covering us to be our authority and power for our ministry and work.

We can see that some people speak with much authority. Actually, the secret is in the Spirit. Before speaking, these people usually exercise their spirits by calling on the Lord, in order for them to be fed within. Then when they come to the meeting, they release their spirits. The more they speak, the crazier they become. Finally, the economical Spirit is poured out upon them so that people receive whatever they speak. This is because they are filled with the Spirit and mingled with God. They have God inwardly and outwardly, in every part of their being.

Real Christians are people who are united and mingled with God. In the past twenty to thirty years, we have published many books speaking about this very matter. I hope that we all would really get into the truth and then go to our relatives and friends to speak the truth. We must speak Christ to people, and we must be "crazy" toward them, telling them that everything else is poor and that Jesus is the best. We should all be "crazy" Christians of this kind who are full of Jesus and full of the Spirit.

THE ULTIMATE CONSUMMATION OF THE DIVINE DISPENSING

Today we enjoy the Lord as the Spirit in our spirit. There will be a day in the future when the Lord will come back to transfigure our body. This will be the redemption of our body. At that time He will come forth from us as glory, and we will also enter into glory (Phil. 3:20-21). Then we will be with Him in the millennial kingdom, enjoying His joy, His presence, His glory, and His authority for a thousand years (Matt. 25:21, 23; Rev. 20:4, 6). After a thousand years of being beside ourselves, a condition that will be full of glory, we will arrive with the Lord at the ultimate manifestation—the New Jerusalem. The New Jerusalem is the ultimate expression of the mingling of God and man—God living in man and man living out God's glory.

This is the central mystery in the Bible. This central mystery is that the Triune God is working Himself into tripartite man so that God and man can be mingled and become one—God in man and man in God. This is a mystery that cannot be described with human words. We absolutely believe that in that day when we are in the New Jerusalem, we will all be "crazy" and beside ourselves because we will all be exulting without end.

Although the millennial kingdom and the New Jerusalem have not come, today in the church life we can have a foretaste of this in miniature. When we call on the Lord, speak the Lord, and enjoy the Lord, we become beside ourselves and are filled with the Triune God inwardly and outwardly.

PREACHING THE CENTRAL MYSTERY AS THE GOSPEL

For this reason, we must speak the truth of the central mystery in the Bible everywhere. We should no longer speak the superficial gospel of peace and prosperity. Do not tell others that if they are suffering, they should believe on Jesus so that they will have peace, or that if their business is bad, they only have to believe in Jesus and pray to Him, and then they will get rich. That is not the gospel. The proper gospel is to tell others that the only God, who is the Triune God—the Father, Son, and Spirit—became flesh, died on the cross to accomplish redemption, and resurrected to become the life-giving Spirit. This life-giving Spirit is the processed Triune God. He went through incarnation, death, and resurrection to become the all-inclusive Spirit. When man repents and believes into Him, immediately He enters into man to be man's life and life supply. He is in man as the essential Spirit and upon man as the economical Spirit. In this way He becomes one spirit with man and man also becomes one spirit with Him. The result is that man possesses real joy, satisfaction, and the true meaning of human life. This is the high gospel that we should announce everywhere.

When we preach and speak in this way, the essential Spirit will fill us inwardly, and the economical Spirit will fill us outwardly. In other words, we will have the Spirit within and without. We will become one spirit with God and will be filled with God. At this juncture, the life we live will be a life of love, light, holiness, and righteousness, and we will spontaneously live out God's image. This is true spirituality, true holiness, and true overcoming. Ultimately this is glory, which will expand to become the kingdom, consummating in the New Jerusalem. This will be the completion of the truth of God's central mystery.

A PRAYER

Lord, we truly worship You for clearly revealing to us all these divine mysteries. Lord, You are God, the Triune God—the Father, the Son, and the Spirit, yet You have worked Yourself into us. Lord, we really praise You. Today You are one with us, and we are also one spirit with You. As the all-inclusive, life-giving Spirit, You dwell in our regenerated spirit, daily sanctifying us, renewing us, transforming us, and conforming us to Your image. One day You will come out of us in glory, and You will also bring us into glory. Lord, we worship

You. What a blessing this is! What a mystery this is! What a glorious economy this is! Lord, bless this word by bringing all the saints into the mysteries of the truth so that we may daily learn this truth, speak this truth, and teach others regarding this central mystery in the Word. Amen.

CHAPTER FIVE

EXPERIENCING AND MINISTERING CHRIST

Concerning the truth, we need to understand and explain it. Concerning Christ, we need to experience Him and minister to others what we have experienced. The Christ we are referring to here is not the objective Christ who is sitting in the heavens but the subjective Christ who is our life. Hence, to experience Christ is to experience life, and to minister Christ is to minister life.

LEARNING TO CUT STRAIGHT AND TO SPEAK THE WORD OF THE TRUTH

Today among Christians there is a lack related to both the truth and to Christ. Most preachers can cover many topics in their sermons, but it is difficult for them to definitely present a particular truth to people. For example, most preachers cannot give people a precise definition of incarnation. In addition, even when a clear and precise definition of incarnation is presented, most people still forget what they have heard right away. For this reason we have to study the truth again and again and practice speaking it until we are so familiar with it that we can speak it accurately even in our dreams. For instance, when we speak about God's attributes, the sequence should be love, light, holiness, and righteousness; we should never reverse the order. This is clearly explained in detail in the life-studies and the footnotes of the Recovery Version of the New Testament. Note 3 of 1 John 1:5 says that love is the nature of God's essence, and light is the nature of God's expression. In other words, love is the essence and light is the expression. Love is first and light is second, because love is God's essence and light is His expression.

Holiness is related to God's nature, and righteousness is related to God's move. God's nature is holy whereas His move, His actions, are righteous. Therefore, holiness is before righteousness.

This requires us to learn and study the truth in a serious way. We must learn to differentiate between love and light and between holiness and righteousness, and we must also speak these things accurately. For example, suppose you go to a restaurant and order a meal that costs twenty dollars. After ordering, you pay the cashier one hundred dollars, and he gives you back ninety dollars. Suppose that after receiving the ninety dollars, you take it as if nothing had happened, eat and drink your meal as usual, and then go home and boast of what happened and show off to your family. This kind of behavior would not be related to holiness but to righteousness. If you take something that costs twenty dollars, but you pay only ten dollars, this is the same as stealing ten dollars. This kind of act is unrighteous. Let us use another example. Suppose you go to a restaurant and buy some food. In addition, you also buy some cigarettes and wine. Then you eat, smoke, and drink to your heart's content. Although this is not something unrighteous, it is unholy. God would never approve of drinking and smoking, because He is holy, and He would never take advantage of people, because He is righteous. Hence, we speak first of His holiness and then of His righteousness.

Love, light, holiness, and righteousness are virtues to man. To God, however, they are attributes. In His human living, the Lord Jesus expressed love, light, holiness, and righteousness as His human virtues. In His divinity He also had love, light, holiness, and righteousness, but they were not expressed outwardly. Rather, they were hidden inwardly as His divine attributes, the rich content of His virtues. For instance, both a glove and a hand have five fingers, but the five fingers of the hand are the inner enriching content, while the fingers of the glove are the expression. The five fingers of the glove are for the outward expression, for a nice appearance. Thus, they are like the human virtues. The five fingers of the hand are hidden in the glove; they are not for a nice appearance but for the rich content. Hence, they are like the divine attributes. The five fingers of the hand, as the attributes, are hidden in the five fingers of the glove to enrich and strengthen the glove. Hence, what is seen outwardly are virtues, and what is hidden inwardly are attributes.

The ancient Chinese sage Confucius also talked about morality and virtues, but the virtues that he taught were not enriched and strengthened with the divine attributes. In the end they were like a glove without a hand inside, having five empty fingers. The virtues referred to in the Bible have the divine attributes as their content and are thus enriched, strengthened, and excelling. This is similar to a glove with a hand inside it. The Lord Jesus was God yet man. He was God, and He was man, so He was a God-man. He was a man with humanity, and He was God with divinity. In His humanity were virtues, and in His divinity were attributes. His human virtues contained His divine attributes, and His divine attributes enriched His human virtues. Because of the strengthening of His divine attributes, His human virtues were enriched. This is the highest standard of morality—the morality of the God-man. The Lord Jesus had such a living on the earth—the God-man living.

PROPER KNOWLEDGE ISSUING
IN SUBJECTIVE EXPERIENCE

Merely having the truth without experience is vanity; hence, we all need to have experience. What is the truth? The truth is God, and God is Christ. Hence, concerning the truth, we cannot have just the doctrinal knowledge; we must also have the experience. In other words, we must experience Christ. For instance, you may tell people that Christ possessed humanity, in which were human virtues, including the virtues of love, light, holiness, and righteousness. You may also tell them that Christ also possessed divinity, in which were the divine attributes, including the attributes of love, light, holiness, and righteousness, and that since Christ had the divine attributes, the human virtues that He expressed were excellent. However, they might ask you, "What does that have to do with me?" If they ask this, you can tell them, "Man was created in God's image. Since you are a man, you were created in God's image, but you do not have God in you. God is a God of love, light, holiness, and righteousness, so you also have the virtues of love, light, holiness, and righteousness. Yet these virtues are like the five fingers of a glove, which are soft and limp. This is because you do not have God inside of you. However, God was within the Lord Jesus as the rich content of love, light, holiness, and righteousness. You need to receive this Jesus into you. He died for you, was resurrected, and has become the life-giving Spirit. This Spirit is Jesus Christ, God Himself. Once you call upon the name of the Lord Jesus, this Spirit will enter into you, that is, God will enter into you. Then His real love, light, holiness, and righteousness will fully enrich your love, light, holiness, and righteousness." This kind of speaking will stir up their inward need.

To make it easier for people to experience and apply these truths subjectively, we may use the following illustration. Suppose a person loves his wife very much. This love was created by God, but his human love cannot last long. Once his wife becomes angry and gives him a long face, his human love falls short. This proves that man's love is like the soft, limp fingers of a glove; it is not enriched and is without the strengthening and supply of God's love. However, if a person receives Jesus Christ as the life-giving Spirit, he will have God. God's love will be in his love, and as a result, he will be able to love his wife, regardless of how she treats him. In other words, as an empty "glove," he will be filled with God as the "hand." With the real fingers inside, the glove's fingers are enriched and strengthened. In the same way, now he will be able to express an excellent love. Just like the person in this illustration, we have patience, which was created by God, that is like the fingers of an empty glove. We also need to receive God into us. Once we do, He will become the patience in us to enrich and strengthen our patience. In the end our patience will be strengthened just as the empty fingers of the glove are made firm when they are filled with the fingers of the hand. God's patience will be put into our patience, and the patience that we express will be an excellent virtue. Therefore, in order to have excellent virtues, we must have the divine attributes within us.

THE URGENT NEED TO LEARN THE TRUTH

I hope that all the saints, especially the young people, would learn the truth in this way. Paul said that God desires all men to be saved and to come to the full knowledge of the truth (1 Tim. 2:4). We should no longer be like the elderly church members in Christianity who have been saved for decades but are still ignorant of the truth. For example, many Christians have been saved for years yet are not clear about the meaning of the name Jesus Christ. Some may think that *Jesus* is the same as *Christ* and that Christ is the Savior. If you ask them what the difference is between the terms *Redeemer* and *Savior,* they probably think that the two terms are nearly the same in meaning. Even many of the saints among us may not know their intrinsic significance and hidden mystery. I do not mean to expose other people's weaknesses, but I want to show you that we are too much under the influence of the old Christian traditions. Although we have spoken many high truths in the past, we have never precisely defined the meaning of the name Jesus Christ. The result is that we probably know something about the meaning but are not altogether sure about it. This is the general situation of Christians today.

In brief, *Jesus* means "Jehovah the Savior." In detail, the Hebrew word for *Jesus* is composed of two words. The first word means "Jehovah" and the second word means "Savior." Hence, *Jesus* means "Jehovah the Savior." This is the clear definition of the name Jesus. The word *Christ* means "God's Anointed." Thus, *Jesus Christ* means that Jehovah the Savior is God's Anointed.

The advantage of a school education is that every thing and every matter are given precise definitions, so that we can learn the proper definitions for things that we know only in a general way. If a person does not quite understand the definitions of various things, his speaking concerning them will not be so definite and accurate. When people listen to him, they will know that he has not received much education. Today

Christians go to church every week, worshipping God fifty-two times a year, yet after ten or twenty years they still may not be certain about biblical truths. Almost none of them can explain the meanings of love, light, holiness, and righteousness. This is why Christians today are so weak and so poor. It is because they have not been properly educated.

The churches in the Lord's recovery must learn from this. Every saint in every church should be educated in the truth. There is a hymn which says that the church is not a school or a factory but an organic garden of God for growing Christ (*Hymns*, #1237). What we do in this garden is the work of planting and watering. However, we should not open a school to teach the Bible. Rather, Bible education should be carried out in the homes. The parents, the older generation, should teach the children, the younger generation. In ancient times the Jews did not have schools. Their education was conducted in their homes with the parents bearing the responsibility of teaching their children. Although the church is not a school but a family, it still needs to carry out the function of teaching. We should receive education in the church, not in the way of school education but in the way of home education—parents teaching the older brothers and sisters, and the older brothers and sisters teaching the younger ones. Eventually, everyone will know how to speak and teach. In this way the church will be filled with the atmosphere of mutual learning and mutual teaching, and all the saints will make much progress in the truth.

These days I am very happy because while traveling through Japan, South Korea, Taiwan, and the Philippines, I have observed that the young people in the churches are pursuing the truth. They can teach one another and even teach the elderly saints. They are able to tell people definitely that Jesus is Jehovah the Savior and that Christ is God's Anointed, because they have learned these things from the life-studies. In the past the old doctrines we preached were like clouds and fog floating in the air—nothing was definite. But now the life-study messages present the truth in a clear and precise way, so that people can readily understand the truth after reading them. So from now on, we have to change our family tradition. We must not be influenced by confused Christianity any longer; instead, we should completely renounce all the old practices. This does not mean that we should discard the Bible but that we should come out of the clouds and fog. We desire to have a clear sky with every truth having a clear definition. We have to learn until we thoroughly understand and are able to speak to others what justification is, what sanctification is, what renewing is, and what transformation is.

LEARNING THE TRUTH
TO EXPERIENCE AND MINISTER CHRIST

After we have learned the truth, we still have to experience Christ so that He may become our reality. In this way, when we speak to people, we will not give them knowledge or doctrines, but we will minister Christ to them. For instance, if we tell people about the benefit of Coca-Cola yet do not give them a can of Coca-Cola to drink, then no matter how interesting our speaking is, they will not be able to enjoy the benefit of Coca-Cola. This is mere speaking without supply. In the past we mostly knew only to supply but not to speak; that also was wrong. The proper practice is that we would all learn to speak Christ and minister Christ to others.

Acts 5:42 tells us that the early disciples announced the gospel of Jesus as the Christ; this means they announced Jesus Christ as the gospel. What they announced was not an empty doctrine nor an elusive gospel but a living Jesus Christ, who is the reality and content of the gospel. After their preaching, once men received the gospel, they spontaneously received Jesus Christ.

In Ephesians 3:8, Paul said that he announced to people the unsearchable riches of Christ as the gospel. This means that Paul did not announce some doctrines; rather, he supplied them practically with the riches of the Lord Jesus Christ. For example, Paul told us that Christ has both divinity and humanity (Rom. 1:3-4). This means that He was God and man, possessing all the divine attributes and human virtues. This is an item of the riches of Christ. Moreover, He also passed through human living, experienced all the trials and ordeals of human life, and endured all the pains of humanity. Then He went to the cross and died, and in His death He terminated all things and accomplished redemption for us. After His death, He resurrected and became the life-giving Spirit. This life-giving Spirit is the Triune God, comprising the Father, the Son, and the Spirit. All the attributes of the Father, the Son, and the Spirit, including love, light, holiness, righteousness, life, power, authority, peace, and joy, are items of the unsearchable riches. However, how can all these riches become our practical experience? How do we minister such a Christ to others in our speaking?

We must tell people that this Christ, who possesses all these unsearchable riches, is now the life-giving Spirit. He is the Redeemer who has accomplished redemption for us, and He is the Savior who is waiting to save us. This Spirit, being omnipresent, is in our heart and in our mouth. As long as we confess, repent, and call upon the name of the Lord Jesus, opening our mouth and believing in our heart, the Spirit will enter into us. When the Spirit comes into us, He comes with all His riches. From then on, as long as we call on Him, breathe Him, and enjoy Him day by day, all His riches will become our experience, and His attributes such as love, light, holiness, and righteousness will become our virtues. Then we will realize that our love is boundless, our patience is enduring and transcendent, and our power is strong. After speaking to people, we should also pray with them. Once they pray, the Spirit will come into them and enable them to touch the reality and comprehend and receive Christ. This is the way to minister Christ to people. First, we should speak the truth and present Christ clearly to them. Then we should pray with them to supply them practically in spirit with what we spoke to them, so that they can receive the Christ whom we have announced.

THE INCREASE OF THE CHURCH DEPENDING ON THE SPREAD OF THE TRUTH

The slow increase in the churches is due to the fact that we do not know how to speak the truth or how to minister Christ. We do not know how to present Christ clearly as the

Romans 10:9-10 That if you confess with your mouth Jesus as Lord and believe in your heart that God has raised Him from the dead, you will be saved. For with the heart there is believing unto righteousness and with the mouth there is confession unto salvation.

EXPERIENCING AND MINISTERING CHRIST   63

truth to people, nor do we know how to supply them with Christ as the living Spirit. This is why after all these years it has been difficult for us to have people remain in the church. I hope that from now on we all would spend time to learn the truth and minister Christ to others for the multiplication and spread of the church.

For instance, as college students you probably have thirty to forty classmates in your class. You can find at least two or three friends from these to talk to about the truth. College students like to listen to the truth. If you do not preach the truth but only chat with them, talking about all sorts of topics every day, when you graduate after four years, you will not have brought anyone to the Lord. You must make a change now and redeem the time. Aside from time for your school-work, you should not waste any time but always seize every opportunity to speak the truth to your classmates. The more clearly you present the truth, the more they will enjoy it. They will also respect you because you know the Bible and Christ. Perhaps they have attended mass in the Catholic Church for twenty years or have been to Sunday services in the denominations for more than ten years, but they may have never heard the things that you speak to them. As long as you speak Christ in a clear, well-founded, and logical way, they will take your word seriously.

We have to thoroughly and comprehensibly explain to people the truths concerning redemption and salvation. Redemption and salvation are two aspects. Redemption resolves the problem of our sins, redeems us back to God, and deals with the problem of our position. It includes forgiveness, cleansing, justification, reconciliation, and acceptance by God. Salvation is related to God's purpose and includes God's regenerating, sanctifying, renewing, transforming, and conforming us into His image. In addition, it also includes His glory eventually being manifested from within us for our full glorification. The more clearly we speak this, the more people will enjoy it, and in the end they will be subdued by us and will appreciate and respect what we speak.

If the young people would speak to their classmates in this way, they would build up some credibility among them and gain their respect and trust. If we cut straight the truth and reveal the light of the Word to them, they will spontaneously show their respect, and the Holy Spirit will also work in them. When we speak to people, the Holy Spirit will touch them, causing them to feel convicted and then to repent, confess, and pray unto their salvation. Thus, to lead people to be saved is not a hard thing. If we do not know how to speak the truth, we may only tell people, "Our church is really good; when we sing, everyone shouts 'Hallelujah' joyfully, and when people share, everyone says 'Amen.'" However, if someone asks us why we do this, I am afraid that we will not be able to give an answer because we may not be clear ourselves. Then these people will have no way to believe.

We must practice this matter with wisdom. Do not say too much at a time. For example, in the four years of college you will have some classmates who attend classes and study with you. You can plan how to speak to them one by one. Perhaps in the first two months you will not find a good opportunity, but you can speak a little. Gradually they will notice that your Bible knowledge is advanced and that your knowledge of the truth is very clear. At this time, whenever there is a chance, you have to open the Bible and speak to them. You can tell them that God created man in His image, that as a result of this we all have God's image, and that we are not ordinary but noble people because we were created in God's image. They will surely be surprised upon hearing this and will want to hear more. Then you can speak to them little by little every time you see them. If you do this, one by one, your classmates will be saved through you.

We should do this not only in the schools but also with our neighbors. In time, all our neighbors will realize that we are those who know the Bible, who are clear about the truth, and who experience Christ. They will sense that we are well-behaved and have a high character, so they will respect our speaking. Once we open our mouths, they will regard highly what we speak. Eventually, surely some will be saved. We should also speak to our parents and relatives in this way. Once they respect and trust us, it will not be too difficult for us to bring them to salvation. This is the way to minister the truth to people and to bring them to the Lord.

I hope that we all can bring one person to the Lord each year. Do not think that this way of increase is very slow; it is, in fact, very fast. Take Taipei as an example. Now there are five thousand saints in the church in Taipei, and the population of the city of Taipei is two million. There are three hundred and sixty-five days, or fifty-two weeks, in a year. It would be very easy for every saint to lead one person to be saved each year. In this way, we will double our number each year. Then in less than ten years we will have gospelized the whole city of Taipei.

We have already pointed out that the church is God's garden. Since it is a garden, it surely has to bear fruit. Suppose there is a fruit tree which bears only one piece of fruit a year, either one banana or one mango. If we saw this, would we be happy or sad? The increase is so slow because we do not know how to speak the truth. If we cannot even explain the names *Jesus* and *Christ* clearly, how can we touch people? If we merely rely on gospel meetings, we will waste our energy, and in the end, people will not want to come. We can no longer rely on evangelizing campaigns or gospel meetings. Instead, we should all speak the truth. We all should speak to our classmates, neighbors, and relatives. Do not speak too much at a time, but speak to them little by little, twice a week. One time you may tell them that man was created in God's image, the next time you may tell them about man's fall, and then you may speak of Christ's redemption and God's dispensing.

For instance, in the beginning we may simply tell people, "You are very good, but have you ever lost your temper? If we always murmur and envy people, this proves that we are fallen sinners. However, God was incarnated to become a man who possessed both divinity and humanity. He is the God of love, light, holiness, and righteousness. If we believe in Him and receive Him, we will be able to live out the human virtues of love, light, holiness, and righteousness. Therefore, we must believe in Him and receive Him." If we speak to people like this twice a week, I believe that after some time we will surely bring one person to salvation.

However, the key is that we lead people to pray and call on the name of the Lord Jesus. We have to tell them, "Today the Lord is the real and living Spirit, and He is in your mouth. As long as you are willing to repent, open your mouth to call on Him, pray to Him, and believe in Him, He will enter into you and bring you into the experience of all His riches." Eventually, you will not only lead one person to salvation in a year but perhaps four to five people. This kind of increase would be tremendous.

In short, the reason we cannot lead people to the Lord is that we do not know how to speak the truth or minister Christ. Hence, much of our labor is in vain. Now I hope that we all would be awakened, would rise up to learn the truth, and would experience Christ. Only the truth can subdue and gain people. We have to learn, starting with the basics and going on to understand the fundamental truths and to study the deeper truths. If we do this, I believe that in five years we will become a group of wonderful saints who will not only know how to speak the truth but also will be able to minister Christ to people through the Spirit, to pray with them, and to open their eyes that they may also gain Christ and receive Jesus as their Savior. In this way the church will be able to gain the increase.

REDEEMING THE TIME TO LEARN THE TRUTH

I hope that not one among us would say that he does not have time. Some people say that they are really busy, but once they get on the telephone, they spend half an hour to an hour gossiping. If we would save our time to learn the truth, we would have more than enough time. It is very easy for us to waste time in our daily life. Hence, Paul told us to redeem the time (Eph. 5:16; Col. 4:5) and understand what the will of the Lord is (Eph. 5:17). To redeem the time means to grasp every opportunity, and the way to redeem the time is to not make any casual telephone calls, to not gossip, and to not waste time. Instead, we should save all our time to learn the truth.

In the past when someone wanted to learn the truth, it was not that easy for him to find reference books, but now there are many spiritual publications among us, and most of

EXPERIENCING AND MINISTERING CHRIST

them are related to the truth. If we have the desire to enter into the truth, there is no lack of reference books, and they are not difficult to get into. As long as we are willing to put in the effort, soon we all will be able to speak the truth. I hope that we all would meet the Lord's demand and make such a vow, so that from today onward we will save our time by not gossiping, not making unnecessary telephone calls, and not wasting our time. Rather, we would endeavor to use the time to learn the truth, to know the truth, to speak the truth, to experience Christ through the truth, and to minister Christ to people by the Spirit. If we do this, the Lord will be able to gain a broad and opened way in every place.

CHAPTER SIX

THE SECOND GREAT PILLAR
IN THE LORD'S RECOVERY—LIFE

Scripture Reading: John 10:10b; 11:25a; 1 John 1:2; 3:9; 5:12; Col. 3:4a; Gal. 2:20; 1 Cor. 15:45b; Rom. 8:2; Col. 1:19; Eph. 4:15, 13; 2 Pet. 1:3-4

THE LORD JESUS BEING THE TRUTH AND THE LIFE

The Lord's recovery is mainly founded upon four pillars: the truth, life, the church, and the gospel. The reason Christianity is degraded is that it has lost the truth and is short of life. The Bible tells us that the Lord Himself is the truth and the life. In John 14:6 the Lord Jesus said, "I am the way and the reality and the life." In this verse the reality is the truth. Thus, the Lord said that He Himself is the life and the truth.

Both the truth and the life are the Lord Himself, but they are two different aspects of what He is. The difference is that the truth is an outward definition and explanation, and life is the inward and intrinsic content. The Lord is in us as our life, but the experience of life needs an explanation. This explanation is the truth. If we receive the Lord according to this explanation, we have life. Hence, in order to experience and enjoy the Lord as life, we must know the truth. The experience of the Lord as life is contained in the Lord as the truth. If we are not clear about the truth and do not understand or know the truth, we will have no way to enjoy the Lord as our life. For this reason we must spend an adequate amount of time to learn the truth.

EXPERIENCING LIFE BY KNOWING THE TRUTH

The Lord has not left us in darkness. Today all of His truths are contained in the Bible, which He has given to us. We must realize that the Bible is a book of life. The reason the Bible is a book of life is that its entire content is truth. All experienced Christians confess that no one can enjoy Christ as life if he does not know the Bible or understand the truth in the Bible. We need to go to the supermarkets to buy food for our physical body to be fed and sustained. In like manner, we must come to the Bible to receive the truth that is in it if we want to receive and enjoy the Lord as life. All the truths in the Bible are food for our spiritual life.

The Bible is not merely a book of knowledge. All the knowledge contained in the Bible is in fact truth, and in this truth, life is concealed. When we read the Bible, if we study only the letter but not the intrinsic truth within, we will not receive life. Hence, every Bible reader has to see the truth that is conveyed through the letter of the Word. Once we see the truth, we will spontaneously touch life. The life-studies have been published to help us enter into the depths of the letter of the Word. Therefore, all those who carefully study the life-studies will surely gain a certain amount of experience. The life-studies bring us into the biblical truths, from which we may receive the genuine life supply.

Today the Lord's recovery is a recovery of the truth and of life. We all know that the decline of Christianity is due to the fact that it has lost both the truth and life. This loss of the truth and life eventually produced many human methods and worldly organizations, which are not what the Lord wants. The Lord does not want any organization or human method. Instead, He wants His church to know Him as the truth and to receive and enjoy Him as life. The entire content of the church must be the growth of Christ in us as truth and life. This may be likened to an orchard, the entire content of which is the fruits of life produced from the fruit trees. In an orchard we cannot find any organization or behavior. We can only see the fruit trees growing and bearing fruit as the issue of their growth in life. This should be the situation of the churches in the Lord's recovery today. In the churches we do not want to have any organization or human methods. Rather, we want to minister to God's people for their growth by planting and watering as the apostle Paul said in 1 Corinthians 3:6 and 9. v. 6 I planted. Apollos watered, but God caused the growth.

v. 9 For we are God's fellow workers; you are God's cultivated land, God's building.

PARTAKING OF THE DIVINE LIFE AND NATURE

We must realize that the church is different from human society and distinct from all the different Christian organizations. The difference or distinction is that human society and Christian groups rely on organization and human work, but the church relies solely on the light of the truth for the enjoyment of the Lord's life. Truth and life are nothing less than the living Lord. The Lord told the disciples, "I have come that they may have life and may have it abundantly" (John 10:10). He even said, "I am the resurrection and the life" (11:25). He is not only the life but also the resurrection. This means that the life, which He is, is resurrection life. The fact that this life is resurrection life means that this life is able to swallow up death. If this life is put into death, death will not be able to overcome it. Instead, because this life is resurrection, it will swallow up death. This resurrection is the Lord Jesus, the One we believe in and receive. Today the Lord Jesus is the Spirit of life who is living and who enlivens and strengthens us. Hence, He is the life-giving Spirit (1 Cor. 15:45b). He is in us to give us life and to supply us day by day that we may grow.

In the six thousand years of human history, there have been many famous philosophers such as Confucius of China and Socrates of Greece who were exceedingly wise and who had many deep and profound thoughts. None of them, however, had the boldness to say that he was life. The statement "I am the life" is very simple yet exceedingly great in its significance. Who can say such a word? If today someone were to tell us, "I am the life," we would surely think that this person was either a fool or insane. What kind of a person can make such a statement? We cannot find a statement like this in all the books and classics throughout human history. Who said such a word? Jesus Christ did. He would not have been able to speak such a word unless He possessed exceptional wisdom and extraordinary reality.

The Lord not only said, "I am the life," but He also said, "I am the resurrection." Moreover, He said, "I have come that they may have life." If He were not God and the ever-living Spirit, and if He did not possess supreme and extraordinary wisdom, how could He have said such a word? This word is simple but mysterious. Just by this word we ought to believe that the Lord Jesus is extraordinary and far superior to Confucius and Socrates. No one has ever had the boldness to say that he is life. Only the Lord Jesus said it, and He even said it repeatedly. He could say this because only He is really the life. He is so great and so transcendent.

After the Lord said this word, He fulfilled it. After He said, "I am the life," Peter, one of His disciples, heard this word and received it. From that time on Peter had the transcending life. He was a fisherman from Galilee, an uneducated man and a layman (Acts 4:13), but after he received this transcendent life, he became a transcendent person. Later, in 2 Peter he wrote, "His divine power has granted to us all things which relate to life and godliness...through which He has granted to us precious and exceedingly great promises that through these you might become partakers of the divine nature" (1:3-4). If Peter had not experienced all these things, he would not have been able to write such a word. He was a Galilean fisherman, yet he was able to say that he was one who received God's life and partook of God's nature.

Today many families like to have dogs and to play with them. However, I do not like dogs because no matter how good they are, they do not have the human nature. I like my grandchildren. Some of them are seven or eight years old, and others are just two or three years old. They scream and crawl on the floor. I enjoy seeing them, playing with them, and letting them lean on me. However, if I saw a puppy in the house, I would immediately drive it out because we are not of the same species. I am a man, and it is a dog. It does not have my human nature, and I do not have its dog nature. The two of us cannot communicate. However, my grandchildren and I are of the same nature. When they call me, "Grandpa!" my heart leaps with joy. When I embrace them, they are happy.

As Christians we have the divine nature and are able to fellowship with God. This is truly a marvelous matter. The reason we have God's life and nature is because Jesus Christ came into us and dispensed God's life into us. From that time on, we have had the sense that we are very close to God and may spontaneously call Him, "Abba, Father!" When we call on Him in such a way, we sense sweetness, joy, and comfort within. The more we call on Him, the more we sense that He is living in us and that we belong to Him. This is because we have His life and nature. We can live by His life and enjoy His divine life.

CHRIST BEING IN US AS OUR LIFE

We are human beings, yet we have God's life and God's nature. Although we are humans, we have become children of God by the life of God. Unfortunately, Christianity has lost this truth and does not teach this truth. Rather, it teaches many insignificant minor items. The United States is the most superior and powerful nation in the world. It is first-class in almost all concepts except in the matter of the truth. Twenty years ago I came to America and spoke using the diagram of the three circles. This diagram covers the three parts of man—the spirit, the soul, and the body. When I spoke about the human spirit, many American Christians and even some preachers said that they had never seen in the Bible that man has a spirit. They knew that there was the Holy Spirit and the evil spirits, but they did not know that man has a spirit. For this reason, I spoke to them everything that is related to the human spirit from Genesis to Revelation. As a result, they were fully convinced.

Some people say that no one ever told the American Christians that man has a spirit. This saying is in fact not accurate because in the last one hundred years in America a few famous spiritual authors have mentioned the human spirit in their writings. For example, the diagram of the three circles is taken from the book *God's Plan of Redemption*, written by an American sister, Mary E. McDonough. When you open this book, you will see the diagram of the three circles. Although the author of this book was an American, the American Christians never read her book. However, I, a Chinese, read it and quoted it to them in my teaching.

There is a Christian group in Anaheim that strongly opposes our preaching that Christ dwells in us. They say, "Christ is so great, and we are so small; how could He dwell in us? There is no such thing as this. Christ today is sitting on the throne and is not in us. Instead, He has sent the Holy Spirit as His representative to be in us. To say that Christ dwells in us is altogether heretical." The truth they teach is completely distorted because they think that the Holy Spirit in us is merely the representative of Christ. They do not see that the Holy Spirit is the Triune God.

In Galatians 2:20 the apostle Paul clearly said, "I am crucified with Christ; and it is no longer I who live, but it is Christ who lives in me." How can people say that the Christ mentioned in this verse is not Christ Himself but a representative of Christ? In saying this, they are altering the Bible. Paul clearly said that Christ was not only in him but was living in him. This means that Christ was moving and working in him. The New Testament does not say that the Christ who is sitting in the heavens has sent merely a representative to be in us. Instead, the New Testament emphasizes that the Christ who is sitting in the heavens is also within us, that is, in our spirit (Rom. 8:10, 34; 2 Cor. 13:5; Col. 1:27; 3:1; 2 Tim. 4:22). Since He is the life-giving Spirit (1 Cor. 15:45b), the Spirit of life (Rom. 8:2), and the Spirit (2 Cor. 3:17), He is omnipresent. Therefore, He can be at the right hand of God and in our spirit simultaneously. He can be in heaven and on earth at the same time.

CHRIST BEING OUR LIFE

The Lord Jesus said, "I am...the life" (John 11:25). Then Paul said, "Christ our life" (Col. 3:4). This is a more personal way of saying what the Lord said. Christ is not only the life, but He is also our life. We should have the boldness to say that Christ is our life, that He lives in us, and that it is no longer we who live, but it is Christ who lives in us. This Christ, who is our life, lives in us as the Spirit of life. If Christ were not the Spirit, He would have no way to come into us.

The English word *pneuma* is an anglicized Greek word denoting "spirit," "wind," or "air." Some tires have the word *pneumatic* printed on them, indicating that the tires must have pneuma, air, for the car to move. If you drive carelessly and one of the tires is punctured by a nail, you will have a flat tire, and your car will stop moving. Today there are many "deflated" Christians. We need to ask ourselves all the time, "Am I full of pneuma or am I deflated?" We must always be filled with pneuma. If we have a flat tire, we have to go to the gas station to pump it up. Similarly, if we are "deflated" inwardly, we have to turn to our spirit to contact the Lord, who is pneuma, so that we will be filled with pneuma, which is the Holy Spirit.

On the evening of His resurrection, the Lord Jesus came into the midst of His disciples. He did not teach them with a lengthy speech nor instruct them on how to conduct themselves. He did only one thing—He breathed into them. Formerly all the disciples had been discouraged and disappointed, "deflated" to the uttermost. They had entirely lost heart, thinking that the Lord was dead and that they were altogether hopeless. However, when the Lord Jesus came, He breathed into them and said to them, "Receive the Holy Spirit" (John 20:22). This is the holy breath, through which the Lord dispensed Himself into them to be their life and everything.

EXPERIENCING AND ENJOYING CHRIST AS LIFE

Most people in Christianity completely ignore this kind of truth. They focus only on the outward practices and neglect the inward reality. For example, in wedding ceremonies the pastor often teaches the wife to be subject to her husband and the husband to love his wife, and both the bridegroom and the bride nod their heads in agreement. Then they go on their honeymoon. Perhaps on the third day, the wife thinks to herself that her husband is unreasonable and wonders how she can be subject to him? The husband may feel that his wife is inconsiderate, but on the first day he restrains his anger and says nothing. He continues to grit his teeth on the second day, but on the third day he can no longer stand it and loses his temper. If we give people only doctrines without giving them the life supply, they will be powerless.

We can never be subject to our husbands or love our wives by ourselves. If we try to do this, we will definitely lose our temper by the third day. We have to realize that since we are Christians, we have the Lord Jesus in us. He is our life because He is the Spirit of life indwelling us. When our husband or wife gives us a difficult time, we should not look at them, because at that time they will seem very ugly. Rather, we should turn to the Lord and behold Him. We should not try to reason with our husbands or wives but should talk to the Lord Jesus inwardly. We can tell the Lord that if He had not given us our husband or wife, we would not have married him or her, but since He did, He should see how unreasonable they are. I believe that as long as we have a little conversation with the Lord, our anger will be dissipated. After He has completely dissipated our anger and infused us with His fragrance, we will surely be filled with joy. Eventually, not only will we not be angry with our husband or wife, but we will also love them very much.

We all know this truth, but unfortunately, most of the time in our practical daily life it is not Christ who lives but we who are living. When our spouse stares at us angrily, we stare back at him or her. At these times, we forget that we are Christians. We are living instead of Christ. When this happens, we should not be surprised and ask how we could lose our temper so badly. Our "I" is no good; it is a gopher, a scorpion, and a serpent. This is why our living is so weak and feeble. Stanza 1 of *Hymns,* #499 says, "Oh, what a life! Oh, what a peace! / The Christ who's all within me lives. / With Him I have been crucified; / This glorious fact to me He gives. / Now it's no longer I that live, / But Christ the Lord within me lives." A couple may sing this hymn with uplifted spirits and resounding voices in the meeting, but once they go home, they may quarrel about the matter of opening or closing the windows. One may say, "The air circulation is not good in the house, so it is better to open the windows." However, the other one may answer, "We should close the windows, or else I may catch a cold." While they are arguing, their eyes look fiercer and fiercer. They have both forgotten that Christ is their life. Thus, it is no longer Christ who lives but the "I" who lives. I believe that in every Christian home there are many unnecessary things that should be given away. In the United States the department stores advertise their sales every Saturday, and many sisters love to read these advertisements. No matter how loudly they sing in the meeting—"Now it's no longer I that live, / But Christ the Lord within me lives"— when they read the advertisements, it is "no longer Christ but I." A sister may notice that her favorite fabric is being sold at a fifty percent discount and that she has a good amount of savings in her bank account. She may decide to drive to the store and buy it. At this time, the Lord may say, "Don't do it. You have enough clothes already." However, she is still "no longer Christ but I." When she arrives at the department store, the Lord may say again, "Do not buy the fabric. Go home!" Nevertheless she remains "no longer Christ but I." After she enters the store, she may pick up a piece of fabric thinking that its color is beautiful and its quality is very good. At this time, the Lord may say again, "Put it down and go home." However, she may reply, "O Lord, please allow me just this once, and I will never do it again. Just allow me this one time to be no longer Christ but I." Many of us have experiences like this.

In how many of the things in our practical daily living can we definitely say, "It is no longer I but Christ"? Sometimes when the telephone rings, the sisters' ears become attached to the telephone just like a piece of metal attracted to a magnet. They cannot get off the telephone until they have talked for half an hour to an hour. If you ask them to read a life-study message, they will excuse themselves by saying that they do not have time. If you ask them to pray over and read the Bible, they will say that they cannot do it because they are busy with their housework. It is actually not that difficult to experience Christ as life as long as we first converse with the Lord and fellowship with Him in every matter. He is not far from us; He is right inside of us. We should inquire of Him, "Lord, what would You do? Do You want me to do that? If You will do it, I will do it with You. If You will not do it, I also will not do it." Then we will know what we should do immediately. This is to enjoy Christ as life and to enjoy God's nature. In this way we can experience the clear leading of Christ within us in every single matter. We will know that He does not want us to do this thing and that He also does not want us to do that thing. In the end, we will spontaneously live out love, light, holiness, and righteousness. In other words, God's divine attributes will be expressed in our human virtues. This is to live Christ and to express Christ.

THE SECRET OF EXPERIENCING CHRIST AS LIFE

Christ is the Spirit, and this Spirit is in you and me and in our spirit all the time. If we want to talk to our spouse, we should not do it right away. We must first have a little conversation with the Lord, saying, "O Lord, my spouse is here. Do You want me to talk to her? Do You want to talk to her? If You would not talk to her, I would not talk to her either." The Lord can testify that many times this is my practice when I talk to my wife. Quite often when I want to talk to her about something, I have this feeling in my spirit that says, "You should first converse with the Lord and ask Him if He wants to talk." When I inquire of the Lord in this way, eight out of ten times He does not want to talk, so eventually I also will not talk. By this kind of practice we can avoid gossiping and wasting our time, and we can also keep ourselves in spirit. We have to practice this even in our dressing. You should not decide by yourself what you should wear. Instead, you should first ask the Lord, "Lord, do You want to wear this shirt? If You will wear it, I will wear it; but if You will not wear it, neither will I." When you do this, you are living Christ, and the issue is that "it is no longer I who live, but it is Christ who lives in me."

When people come to debate with me concerning certain doctrines, sometimes when my words are on the tip of my tongue, inwardly I am reminded that I must first turn to the Lord. Then I fellowship with the Lord, saying, "Lord, do You want to speak? If You speak, I will speak; if You will not speak, I will not speak either." Eight out of ten times the Lord does not want to speak, so I do not speak either. In the end, many troubles are avoided. This is to live Christ and to enjoy Christ as life. This is a fact, not an empty doctrine. The Lord is real and living, and He is right inside of us. We must always contact Him and have fellowship with Him. Whenever we speak or do anything, we should not do it according to our own decision. Rather, we should first contact the Lord and have fellowship with Him. Even if you have been wronged and want to cry and shed tears, you still have to fellowship with the Lord first, saying, "Lord, will You cry? If You will cry, I will cry. If You will not cry, I will not cry." If we all practice this, the result will be that we will live Christ, and we will experience Christ as life.

The Christ in whom we believe is God, the Lord who created the heavens and the earth. He is the Triune God—the Father, the Son, and the Spirit while at the same time He is our Redeemer and Savior. Today He has become the life-giving Spirit, the Spirit of life, and even the sevenfold intensified Spirit who is in us. We should not neglect Him at any time, but we should always practice having fellowship with Him. Even when we are about to get angry, we should first ask Him, "Lord, I am getting angry. Are You angry? I want to punish my children; do You think I should beat them? I want to scold them; would You scold them?" Once we fellowship with the Lord, we will be enlightened right away. We will see that we do not have any love, light, holiness, and righteousness at all. We will also realize that He is in us as love, light, holiness, and righteousness. When the husband wants to scold his wife, the Lord will immediately be unhappy, and often when the wife wants to buy the merchandise on sale on Saturday, the Lord will withdraw right away. Surely we all have had this kind of experience. Many times although He does not say anything, we know His feeling. Sometimes we may be having enjoyable fellowship with Him, but at a certain point He turns His face away from us. As a result, we realize that He does not agree with us. This is because He is love, light, holiness, and righteousness, and we are not love, light, holiness, and righteousness at all. Eventually, we will be subdued by Him and will do things according to His will. This is the secret of experiencing Christ as life.

The Lord Jesus is the all-permeating Spirit. He is not only on the throne in the heavens but also in us at the same time. Ephesians 3:17a says that He is even making His home in our hearts. Our heart is composed of all the parts of our soul—our mind, emotion, and will—plus our conscience, the main part of our spirit. For Christ to make His home in every part of our heart, He must spread outward, permeating us part by part, and He must also go downward, taking root in us step by step. He is "invading" us all the time. He first enters into our spirit and waits for the most opportune time. Once He has a chance, He enters into our mind. Sometimes we struggle with Him, trying to push Him out, but He is very patient. He keeps struggling to move on, and eventually He "invades" our mind. Then He waits for another opportunity to enter into our emotion and will. We may tell Him, "Lord, don't go so fast. Please slow down." However, the more we say this, the faster He comes. In the end, He "invades" our emotion and will also.

I have been "invaded" by the Lord for more than fifty years. Today there is nearly no room in me left for myself; almost all the room has been occupied by Him. Even though I may not want to say, "It is no longer I but Christ," I still have to say it because He has already occupied my entire being. I do not have any room for myself. Sometimes when I want to do something, immediately the Lord who is in me will say, "You do it yourself; I am not doing it." Ultimately, I also cannot do it because "it is no longer I but Christ." In our practical daily living, is it "I" or is it Christ who lives? May this short and simple fellowship be a constant reminder to us.

CHAPTER SEVEN

PRODUCING AND FEEDING THE LAMBS

THE FATHER'S GLORIFICATION BEING HIS EXPRESSION THROUGH THE MULTIPLICATION OF LIFE

Although each of the four Gospels refers to the matter of gospel preaching, the record in the Gospel of John is the most particular. At the end of Matthew the Lord charged the disciples to preach the gospel (Matt. 28:18-20), and at the end of both Mark and Luke the Lord also gave similar charges (Mark 16:15-16; Luke 24:46-48). In the Gospel of John, however, the Lord did not charge the disciples to preach the gospel. Instead, He told them that He wanted them to bear fruit. The Gospel of Matthew presents the preaching of the gospel of the kingdom, the Gospel of Mark presents the preaching of the gospel to the whole creation, and the Gospel of Luke presents the preaching of the gospel for forgiveness of sins. The Gospel of John, however, is a book, a gospel, concerning life. Hence, in the Gospel of John the preaching of the gospel is mainly not in the way of proclaiming or preaching but in the way of releasing life.

In John 15:4-5 the Lord said to the disciples, "Abide in Me and I in you. As the branch cannot bear fruit of itself unless it abides in the vine, so neither can you unless you abide in Me. I am the vine; you are the branches. He who abides in Me and I in him, he bears much fruit." The branches' abiding in the vine is not merely the preaching of the gospel but the overflowing of the inner life. For example, fruit trees in an orchard do not preach the gospel there; they just grow. Moreover, their full growth is the overflow of the life within them. This overflowing life will practically issue in much fruit. Hence, the fruit-bearing of the branches of the fruit trees is the issue of the overflow of their inner life.

In John 15 we see the same picture. There it says that the Father is glorified in that we bear much fruit (v. 8). Many Christians do not know what it means for the Father to be glorified. The Father's being glorified is His being multiplied. For example, suppose there is a young man who does not have any children after being married for ten years. Thirty years later he still has no children. Finally, when he is ninety years old, he remains barren. If you went to visit him at his home, you would see only an old man with his body bent over and his old wife who can hardly walk. Instead of having a sense of glory, you would have a sense of pity. However, suppose a young man after being married for twenty years has begotten twelve sons and eight daughters, and suppose all of his children also beget sons and daughters after their marriages, giving him fifteen grandchildren. He may be only fifty-five years old, yet he already has numerous offspring. If we saw how many offspring he had, we would admire him and say, "Glorious, glorious! This is really glorious! You have produced so many offspring."

Our Father is glorified in that we bear much fruit. This means that the Father's divine life is expressed through our fruit-bearing as the branches of the vine, and in this He is glorified. When we see so many young people in the church rising up to love and serve the Lord and so many who are being brought into the church, we joyfully exclaim, "Glory!" We exclaim this because the Father's divine life is being multiplied.

Thirty years ago when I first visited the Philippines, some among the responsible brothers at that time looked like trees with hardly any growth, and with some we could not tell whether they were little plants or stones. However, more than twenty years later they are all growing gray. Suppose that in the Philippines there was only a group of such elderly saints. Suppose that there were no young people, not to mention local people, who had been brought into the church, and that even the children of the elderly saints had been lost. If this were the case, our hearts would be frozen. If we heard the elderly saints singing weakly and feebly, we would surely weep and sob because if a church does not have young people, it has no posterity and therefore no future. However, when we see all the young people, especially the new ones, rising up, and when we hear them singing in the meeting, it is really glorious. This confirms what the Lord said: "In this is My Father glorified, that you bear much fruit." If the meeting halls in our localities are filled with young people, what a glory it will be!

For this reason we all need to be reminded that we have to go forth and bear fruit. Every one of us has to make a vow before the Lord that we each will bear one fruit a year. If we cannot bring one person to the Lord; that is, bear one fruit for the Lord in one year (three hundred and sixty-five days), this will be a shame to us. Perhaps week by week we come alone to the meetings with only our Bible and hymnal. Five years ago it was so, and now, five years later, it is still the same—we have not brought one person with us. If this is our situation, then there is no glory at all. However, suppose next spring each of us brings a lamb, and in the second half of the year each one of us brings another lamb. Then we will all have the inward sense that this is glorious. If each of us would bring two lambs by the second half of next year so that all the seats of the meeting hall are filled, then the expression will be even more glorious.

THE PROBLEM OF THE SPIRITUAL LIFE
BEING BARRENNESS

I can testify to you that I have lambs everywhere. This is why I am so happy. Wherever I go, there are flocks of lambs receiving my feeding. When I am feeding them, my heart feels joyful and glorious. I hope that you all would answer the Lord's call, forgetting about everything else and not caring about the situation of the meetings, but you would simply go forth and bear fruit, bringing the lambs into the church life.

I do not mean to incite anyone; I just want to point out the way of life to all of you. The reason we do not have much growth in life is that we are barren. Hence, we must drop all other things and simply go forth and bear fruit. Once we bear fruit, all our sicknesses will be healed spontaneously. Those who are weak will be made strong, while those who are spiritually unhealthy will become normal and healthy.

Every parent has this kind of experience. Sometimes they are very busy and tired and even become sick, but once they see their children, their sickness is gone and all their strength wells up. When a person is sick, he may ask for a leave from his company, but he cannot ask for a leave from his children. Once he sees his children, all his sicknesses will be gone. Similarly, when we see our "lambs," the ones we have led to salvation, our problems will all disappear and our sicknesses, whether physical or spiritual, will all vanish.

Yesterday at lunch, due to a little overeating, I did not feel well and became sick. Last night after I had released the message in the meeting, I took my temperature at home and found that I had a fever. Perhaps I began to develop the fever while I was releasing the message, but for the sake of feeding my lambs I did not take care of myself. It was not until after I had fed my lambs that I was conscious of my rising body temperature. After I took some medicine, my fever was gone. When I got up the next morning, I felt very hungry and did not have any energy. Originally, I had intended to rest that day, but when I remembered that the lambs needed to be nourished, I came to the meeting. As soon as I opened my mouth, my strength welled up. Thus, I deeply believe that when we go forth to bear fruit and shepherd the lambs, all of our sicknesses will be gone and all of our weaknesses will disappear. Moreover, we will surely grow in the spiritual life.

NOT ONLY PRODUCING THE LAMBS
THROUGH FRUIT-BEARING
BUT ALSO FEEDING THE LAMBS

The way John wrote the Gospel of John was very special. He first mentioned in chapter fifteen that we have to go forth and bear fruit. This is related to the plant life. Then in chapter twenty-one he said that we have to feed the lambs (vv. 15-17). This means that the plant life becomes the animal life—each fruit becomes a lamb. It is relatively easy to bear fruit, but it is not that easy to take care of and feed lambs.

Every parent knows that even though it is laborious to give birth to a child, it is still somewhat easy. However, after the child is born, it is not easy at all to raise him up to be an adult. According to John's words, to lead someone to be saved is to bear fruit. Initially, this one is a like a grape; however, after he is saved, baptized, and regenerated to be a child of God, he becomes a lamb that requires much feeding for his growth in life. This is truly a toilsome task.

Today we all desire to lead people to salvation, but once some are baptized, we usually hand them over to the elders of the church to be taken care of. However, a church has only a few elders at most. Even if they are all experienced "mothers," they still cannot take care of so many children. Hence, many of these children either die prematurely or are taken away by others. In the end, we may gain a hundred, yet only five may remain in the church. Time and again many were regenerated through the church's baptism meetings, but after they were baptized, it seems that there was no follow-up care. This was because we were interested in delivering babies, but we neglected to nurture them. In the past the church in Taipei also had the same kind of problem. The church there led many people to be saved and often baptized eighty to ninety people at a time. However, the more people were baptized, the more people were neglected because no one took up the responsibility to take care of them. From now on, every saint in the church has to learn to be a responsible parent and to change the former situation of handing over the new ones. After you give birth to a baby, you should not just hand it over to others; rather, you have to take good care of him and feed him. If you have brought in a new one, you should bear the responsibility to shepherd him. Since he is your baby, you must take care of him and feed him. Only by this way can the new ones be kept and become remaining fruit. If we only lead people to salvation without bearing the responsibility of shepherding them, later we will still have to give an account before the Lord. The Lord's words to Peter clearly reveal that we must shepherd the few lambs that the Lord has committed to us.

FRUIT-BEARING AND LAMB-FEEDING ISSUING IN THE GROWTH AND MULTIPLICATION OF THE CHURCH

While we are fulfilling the obligation of feeding and taking care of the lambs, we will find that our knowledge of the truth is very inadequate and that we need more learning and equipping. At the same time, we will also realize that our experience of Christ is inadequate and that we therefore need to pursue a deeper experience of Christ, just as parents, in taking care of their children, realize their insufficiency and are forced to learn more and practice more. Only this will cause the growth of the whole church.

I do not mean to criticize anyone, but the fact is that the older saints tend to be easily drawn to the old things. All the elderly saints have to realize that the situation today is very different from that of twenty years ago and is altogether different from that of half a century ago. Therefore, do not keep talking about how the situation of the church was in 1934 or in 1964. We should not confine ourselves to the old, traditional ways. Rather, we should just go forth and bear fruit. The Lord's recovery in the Philippines has already had a history of twenty to thirty years, but the number of saints is less than ten thousand, merely .02% of the entire population. Excluding the southern part of the Philippines, we have less than one thousand saints in the whole metropolitan area of Manila. This condition is not a glory but a shame to us. Do not say that the elders should bear this responsibility. There are only a few elders, and even if they exhausted themselves, they still could not bear such a responsibility.

I say this in order to stir you up to go forth and bear fruit. Every saint in the church has to go forth and bear fruit. Once a fruit is produced, it becomes a lamb. We should not be lambs. We should be little shepherds feeding the lambs. If we all take care of our lambs, they will also be influenced by us to go forth to bear fruit and feed the lambs. This will become the family tradition in the Lord's recovery. The church will multiply endlessly and expand and grow year by year. In this way, when people come to the church and see that there are so many new ones growing healthily, they will surely have a glorious feeling.

BEING EQUIPPED IN THE TRUTH
AND GROWING IN LIFE
IN ORDER TO FEED THE LAMBS

The Gospel of John is a book on life, but John was also particularly fond of using the word *truth* in his writings. Hence, in his Epistles, just as in his Gospel, he first mentions the truth and then presents the matter of life. This shows us a spiritual principle. If there is no truth, there will be no life; and if there is no life, there will be no truth.

In John 14:6 the Lord put life and truth together. Then in chapter fifteen the Lord spoke of the matter of fruit-bearing. This indicates that fruit-bearing has a great deal to do with life and truth. Experientially, our barrenness exposes our shortage in life. Why are we barren? It is because we are not rich in life. If we have an abundance of life, we will spontaneously bear fruit. If we would pay attention to fruit-bearing, we surely must pay attention to the growth in life. If we would pay attention to the growth in life, we must also pay attention to pursuing the truth. Once we have the truth, we will be led into the experience of Christ. In this way we will be able to shepherd our lambs. Otherwise, we will have nothing to feed our lambs with and no way to take care of them. Without knowing the truth or growing in life, we may still be able to lead people to be saved and baptized; however, if we lack the knowledge of the truth and the experience of Christ, we will not be able to properly fulfill the responsibility of feeding.

Parents feed their children by giving them food to eat and milk to drink. Similarly, in order to feed our lambs, we must prepare spiritual food and milk. The Lord's word is the bread of life (John 6:35, 63) and the spiritual milk (1 Pet. 2:2). If we know the truth in the Bible and the word of the Lord, we will be able to give our lambs much nourishment. For example, we can use the Gospel of John to feed others, saying, "John chapter one says that the Lord was God, and as God He became flesh. Furthermore, with Him came the truth, which is the Word of God. Then chapter eight says that the truth shall set us free, and chapter seventeen says that we are sanctified in the truth. In actuality, the truth is nothing less the Lord Jesus Himself. Thus, we have to love the Lord, pray to Him all the time, and read His word every day." How good this is! The Gospel of John speaks of life and truth. This life and truth are just the Lord Jesus, and today He is the Spirit who lives in us and supplies us day by day. Hence, chapter six tells us that the Lord is the bread of life for us to eat (vv. 35, 48). When we eat Him, we live because of Him (v. 57).

If we have a rich knowledge of the truth and a considerable measure of the experience of life, when we go to visit our lambs, we will be able to supply them with the milk of the word according to their situation. This is the proper practice of feeding the lambs. Regrettably, when most of us see our lambs, usually we can only say, "Do you attend the Lord's Day meeting? Why don't you come to the meeting? The meeting is really good; you surely have to come." We only know to say this to our lambs over and over again. Eventually, they get so tired of us, and gradually they do not like to see us anymore because they know that we have nothing to say except, "The meeting is really good; please come." This is not feeding them; rather, it is like serving them a summons to appear in court. Therefore, they not only are not supplied, but they even grow tired of us.

Therefore, when we see our lambs, we should not say, "The meeting is really good; please come." Instead, we have to speak the truth to them. The truth is the Lord's word. Perhaps some saints will say, "There are many places in the Word which I do not understand; I cannot even comprehend the Gospel of John." The Lord has already opened the entire New Testament to us in the life-study messages. If someone does not understand the Gospel of John, he should read the *Life-study of John* where all the truths are opened. Once he reads the life-study messages, he will be able to understand the intrinsic significance of the book.

After we have learned the truth and we see our lambs again, we should not say, "The meeting is really good; please come." Instead, we should invite them to read John 1:14 with us: "And the Word became flesh and tabernacled among us...full of grace and reality." Then we may explain to them, "The reality here is the truth, and the truth is the explanation of Christ. This explanation is found in the entire Gospel of John. Verses 31 to 36 of chapter eight tell us that everyone who commits sin is a slave of sin. The truth, however, shall set us free. So we have to pursue the truth, and when we have the truth, the truth shall set us free." This simple word will supply them with a cup of "the milk of the word" and two small pieces of "solid food" that they may be nourished substantially. When they go back, the Holy Spirit will surely work through our speaking, because the Lord's word is spirit, and they will have the Spirit operating in them. Even though we may not ask them to come to the meeting, they will surely come the next time.

Later, we may further speak to them, "The truth not only shall set us free, but it is also an explanation of the Lord. The Lord is life and is inside of us. John 15 says that we have to learn to abide in the Lord and that the Lord will also abide in us. Then we will abide with the Lord mutually. We can enjoy Him, and He can be our life. Eventually, we will be able to bear fruit for the Father to be glorified." If we feed them in this way over and over again, after two or three months they will grow in life, overflow life, bear fruit, and bring people to the Lord. Their fruit will then become their lambs, and they will feed their lambs according to the way they were supplied by us. In this way one link is connected to another—we take care of them as our lambs, they take care of others as their lambs, and their lambs take care of still others as lambs. What a glorious situation this will be. This is the overflow of life and the feeding of life.

THE PRACTICE OF SERVING FULL-TIME

The churches in America have already started a practice in which the college students set apart two years right after their graduation to serve the church. Of course, this is not a regulation but something of the saints' own free will. Once they graduate from college, they learn how to serve in the church. They spend four hours in the morning, five days a week, to focus on reading the life-study messages in order to study the truths in the New Testament. After two years they will have studied the entire New Testament once. In the afternoons they either go to visit people in the homes or to contact students at the campuses. In the evenings they may join the meetings or go out to do the Lord's work. This kind of practice is very effective, and those who serve this way also receive much benefit. After two years the church will decide, according to their performance and desire, as well as according to the Lord's leading, whether or not they should remain full-time or go to get a job.

If the college young people in the Lord's recovery would dedicate two years after their graduation to go forth for the preaching of the gospel and to receive spiritual edification, the future of the Lord's recovery will be immeasurable. In the church there should be some who serve the Lord full-time. In the Lord's recovery, serving full-time does not mean that you enter the profession of preaching and earn your livelihood by preaching. The Bible clearly shows us that this is not necessarily so. For example, Paul was one who served full-time, but in times of need he also made tents (Acts 18:3; 20:34-35). Aquila and Priscilla were also tentmakers by trade like Paul, but they were like full-timers. Wherever they went, they opened their homes entirely for the church and the saints (Rom. 16:3-5a; 1 Cor. 16:19b). Thus, serving full-time is a practice, not a profession. The college graduates can set apart two years and then get a job. After a period of time, if the church has the need or they feel that they should acquire further learning, they can come out to serve full-time again. This kind of practice is living and organic, without any element of regulation.

As a rule, we all should consecrate our time to the Lord. The more time that we consecrate, the better. In particular, there are many housewives among us. During the day most people have to go to work or to school, but these housewives have a lot of time. Thus, they should give their time for the Lord's use. A definite way to do this would be for them to open their homes and invite their relatives and friends to hear the gospel. However, they should not invite the elders to come and preach; instead, they should preach the gospel themselves. Perhaps many of them will try to make an excuse, saying that they are not able to preach the gospel. However, their inability is the exact reason that they need to learn the truth and be equipped with the truth. Please bear in mind that if you invite the elders or the gifted ones to preach the gospel, the result may not be good. Only when you yourself preach and speak will the gospel be living and effective. If all the saints would serve and function—not relying on the gifted ones but diligently learning the truth, experiencing Christ, endeavoring to give their time, opening their homes, and trying their best to preach the gospel—the impact would be great. In Taipei we also mentioned the burden of serving full-time, and surprisingly, many people immediately responded. Now there are about six hundred who have the desire to serve full-time and another six hundred who want to serve part-time. We are full of joy concerning this. These one thousand two hundred saints may be considered the future of the church in Taipei. In the same principle, I hope that there would be an adequate number of people everywhere willing to serve full-time, so that the Lord would have a free way to do whatever He wants to do in every place.

Chapter Eight

THE KEY TO THE REVIVAL OF THE CHURCH

THE LEARNING AND SERVICE
OF THE FULL-TIME SERVING ONES

Some who have served in the church for many years do not know how to lead or help the new full-time serving ones to have a proper equipping and learning before the Lord. Thus, the following three points can be regarded as directions on how to lead the young people in their service.

Learning to Know the Truth

If a young person graduates from college and desires to learn to serve full-time, the first thing he should learn is the truth. Every morning the full-time serving ones should spend much time on the matter of learning the truth through the use of the Recovery Version of the New Testament with its footnotes and references and with the help of the life-study messages. If they spend four hours every morning to do this, they will be able to study the New Testament once in two years. This is a necessary equipping.

Learning to Preach the Gospel

Second, the full-timers must learn to preach the gospel. Not only should they know how to preach the gospel, but they should also help the saints to open their homes for the preaching of the gospel, even to the extent that they would "force" all the saints to open their homes. To do this in a proper way requires the full-timers to exercise wisdom. We have to think of a way to help the saints to open their homes, whether they are strong, weak, or have stopped meeting for a long time. Then we have to help them to invite their relatives, neighbors, colleagues, and classmates, and we also have to lead them in preaching the gospel. They should not ask the elders and co-workers to preach the gospel; rather, they should do the preaching themselves. Once they speak, they will be vitalized and will have the heart to pursue, learn, and be equipped. The best way to recover the saints, especially those who have stopped meeting for a while, is to ask them to preach the gospel to other people. Once they speak, their cold hearts will be rekindled, and they will spontaneously come to the meetings.

Learning to Hold Group Meetings

Third, full-timers must learn how to have small groups. The church has to divide into small groups with eight to twelve people in each group. The full-timers must learn to lead a small group. The secret of leading a small group is that you should not be the one doing everything, but you should only help the saints to form the group. Then you should discuss with them how to take care of the group meeting and how to take care of the saints. As to the principle of grouping, do not group the saints according to their spiritual conditions; instead, group them according to geographical boundaries. For example, if there are eight saints living in a brother's neighborhood, you can arrange for them to come together to form a group. As for the meeting location, they can rotate among their homes after discussing among themselves and agreeing to a proper sequence in rotation.

It is best not to have the title of "group responsible one." Do not ask any particular person to take the lead either. Instead, let everyone in the group take the lead and bear the responsibility of the group. Although it is the full-timer who helps the small group, he is neither the one who calls the meeting nor the one who takes the lead. All the members of the group must take care of and bear the responsibility of all the matters and decisions related to the group.

There are at least one thousand saints in metropolitan Manila. These one thousand saints should establish one hundred small groups. First, you have to take a proper "census" by locating all the saints according to their information cards.

Then, no matter what their spiritual situations are, you have to arrange groups for them. The content of the small group living may consist of gospel preaching, feeding, and edification. If the number of people in a group increases, they can divide into two groups. In this way the church will spontaneously multiply and increase.

LEARNING TO FEED AND TO SHEPHERD

Hence, the full-timers mainly have to do these three things: learn the truth, preach the gospel, and lead the small groups. To lead the small groups is actually to feed the lambs. In John 21 when the Lord spoke of feeding the lambs, He used different words, indicating that different kinds of edification should be rendered to different kinds of people. In verse 15 He said, "Feed My lambs"; in verse 16 He said, "Shepherd My sheep"; and in verse 17 He summed everything up by saying, "Feed My sheep." *Lambs* denotes little lambs, referring specifically to individual lambs whereas *sheep* denotes a flock, referring to the church (John 10:14, 16; Acts 20:28). Feeding means to render the life supply to others, nourishing them with the riches of life; shepherding, on the other hand, is related to the building. We shepherd the saints by feeding them unto the building up of the church (Matt. 16:18; 1 Pet. 2:2-5). Today in the church there are many lambs. In particular, all the brothers and sisters who are not meeting regularly are lambs. There are also some who have been meeting for twenty years but are not grown up; these are the "old lambs." All the full-timers must learn to shepherd these lambs, recover them, and supply them with the guileless milk of the word that they may gradually grow in life. Then the full-timers must continue to shepherd them that they may be built up into a dwelling place of God in spirit (Eph. 2:22).

PROMOTING THE LEARNING OF THE TRUTH

Not only should the full-timers learn these three things, but every saint should also learn them. First, you all have to learn the truth. This requires that you pay the price and make an effort to study carefully. One time I asked the elders what the meaning of *Jesus* is and what the meaning of *Christ* is. It was as if they were all inexperienced, for none of them could give me a clear answer. Since we all have been serving in the church for years, we should not have some who are still inexperienced. Suppose you teach a group of students English, but at the end some of them have not learned anything, and others have learned only half of everything. Would you continue to teach them? Most of the churches in the Lord's recovery are currently in this kind of situation. The majority of the saints have learned only half of the truth, so ultimately no one has learned the truth in a complete way. Thus, there is no way to build up the service and no way for the Lord to go on.

Now that all the life-studies of the New Testament have been published, I hope that all the churches would take this set of books as the basis for their study and greatly promote the learning of the truth. In every church we have to help all the saints to study the Recovery Version of the New Testament, especially the footnotes, in a careful and thorough way. This will truly be a great task. In the past we felt that we had nothing to do. Actually, this was because we did not do anything and did not want to do anything. Even when we truly wanted to do something, we could not find the way to do it, so we lost interest in doing anything. However, now the way has been clearly presented to us, and everything depends on whether or not we are willing to pay the price. If we are willing to pay the price, I believe that in three to five years the whole church will make great progress in learning the truth.

PROMOTING THE SPREAD OF THE GOSPEL WORK

Second, we have to encourage all the saints to preach the gospel from house to house. This will be very effective. All the full-timers should receive the burden to do this. When you go to the saints concerning this matter, do not go to the brothers first, because most of them will say that they do not have the time. You should contact the sisters, who are more likely to receive the burden because their hearts are softer. It is the same with the matter of the small groups—you have to work on the sisters first. Once they are set on fire, it will spread to the brothers, and eventually every home will be opened.

We should also have a good campus work. There should be some who preach the gospel to the college students in every college. This is a crucial work. Furthermore, we must also do the children's work in a serious way because the children are the future of the church. You may want to consider preaching the gospel to the children first. Then, aside from gaining the children of the saints, you must also gain some from the unbelievers. This work is very worthwhile. If these five items—promoting the learning of the truth, preaching the gospel from house to house, shepherding in the group meetings, doing the campus work, and doing the children's work—are properly established, the church life will be living and healthy and will surely increase and multiply.

PURSUING THE TRUTH TO BRING IN THE REVIVAL

In order to serve, we all must be equipped with the truth, and in particular, we all must be familiar with the New Testament. All of you who have the heart to serve full-time must get yourselves fully equipped by studying the life-study messages thoroughly. Otherwise, when you go to establish the work, shepherd people, and speak to people, you will have nothing to say.

In this matter the co-workers should take the lead. We do not force the saints to read the life-studies, but every co-worker should read the life-study messages in a thorough way. In America all the doctors and nurses in the hospitals have to take examinations every year. In Taiwan some organizations also require their employees to take annual examinations. We have never held any examinations for the co-workers, so no one really knows whether they are qualified in the matter of the truth. It seems that once a person becomes a co-worker, he obtains a very secure job, and no one can dismiss him. Some co-workers even think that as full-time serving ones they are special people and that everyone has to listen to them. It is inappropriate and wrong to think this way. From now on we will not allow this kind of situation. Whoever wants to be a co-worker or to continue to be a co-worker must pass through an examination once a year.

Many Christians acknowledge that the churches in the Lord's recovery know the truth the most. However, we have to ask ourselves how many of us are really like this? Actually, the majority of the saints do not know the truth that much. Therefore, I hope that the Lord will be gracious to us by stirring up the churches all over the world to rise up and pursue the truth. I believe that if we endeavor for three to five years, the saints will be revived by studying the Word. This will bring in a big revival on the earth.

I hope that we can stir up this kind of a pursuing atmosphere in the church life. From now on, there should not be any more idle talk in the saints' homes. Even when they converse, they should also study the truth. For example, when you go to a saint's home, you should not just greet him and ask, "How are you?" Instead, you should ask him, "What does the genealogy in Matthew 1 talk about?" You may also go further and ask him, "Do you know that there are three important names in the genealogy in Matthew 1? They are Abraham, David, and Mary. These are three crucial persons who brought in Christ." When you meet a saint on the street, instead of talking to him about other things you should ask him, "Which verse in the Gospel of John says that the Lord is edible? How did the Lord say that He was edible? Why did the Lord say that He was edible?" Thus, in a conversation of just two minutes both of you will be reminded, supplied, and mutually nourished. We have to change the atmosphere and encourage the brothers and sisters to read the life-studies. Even when we are facing matters related to national affairs, such as an election, we still should not talk about them. Let those who belong to Caesar be occupied with Caesar's business. As those who belong to God, we ought to be occupied with God's business (Luke 20:25).

One time I was given hospitality at a couple's home. They were Chinese who lived outside of China and had never studied in a Chinese school, but they spoke very good Chinese. The hostess told me that because she had been meeting and listening to messages in the Lord's recovery for a long time, she had learned Chinese very well. When I listened to her fellowship, however, I realized that she did not know the truth very much. Eventually, I found an opportunity to tell her, "I am really grateful that you gave me hospitality and had three or four suits made for me, but I am very concerned about your spiritual situation. I hope that the next time I come we can talk about the truth." We all should do this to stimulate the lambs in our small group. Do not be afraid of offending others. We may offend someone today and tomorrow, but he will be grateful toward us the day after tomorrow.

OUR WILLINGNESS TO PUT IN THE EFFORT TO PURSUE THE TRUTH BEING MORE IMPORTANT THAN THE WAY WE PURSUE

Someone may ask whether it is necessary to follow a certain sequence in pursuing the truth or whether the method of teaching, reciting, testing, and praying that we used in the past is the proper way to study. Others may ask whether it is proper for the full-timers to study gospel materials such as *Gospel Outlines* in order to preach the gospel. Actually, in pursuing the truth it does not matter which book we study. We may study Matthew, Romans, or Revelation. Basically, every book in the New Testament is all-inclusive, speaking mainly concerning Christ and the church. Hence, we do not need a definite sequence in our pursuing. The crucial thing is that we must be willing to spend an adequate amount of time to study. The full-timers should spend four hours every day in the morning to study. Then they will be able to finish the entire New Testament in two years. The saints who have a heart to pursue can spend at least an hour a day; then they will be able to finish the New Testament in eight years. Some may think that eight years is too long, but when you finish it, you will not feel that it was too long. Bear in mind that you may start from any book. The most important thing is that you must be willing to put in the effort and continue steadfastly.

As for books like *Gospel Outlines,* you can pursue them

when you have extra time. You have to spend all your effort on the study of the Recovery Version of the New Testament and the life-studies. After you have finished all the life-studies, you may get into the materials for gospel preaching. If you have studied the life-studies thoroughly, you will be able to handle all the services in the church. Concerning how to lead the saints, your focus should be to cause the saints to become constituted with the truth and to be able to present the truth using clear logic. Take the book of Romans for instance. The whole book can be divided into four stations, each consisting of four chapters. This has been clearly presented in the life-studies, and you have to make good use of them to help you to memorize these main points.

The book of Romans has four stations. Chapters one through four are the first station, which is justification. Chapters five through eight are the second station, the station of sanctification. Chapters nine through twelve are the third station, the station of the Body of Christ, because chapter twelve says that as members the believers are becoming one Body. Chapters thirteen through sixteen are the last station, the station of the church life, because chapter sixteen mentions the local churches in different places, such as the church in Cenchrea, the church in the home of Priscilla and Aquila, and the churches of the Gentiles.

In the past nineteen centuries many people have studied Romans, but none of them was able to say that the last station of this book is on the local churches. The book of Romans is concerning the gospel of God (1:1-4). As sinners, we need justification and then sanctification. Sanctification is transformation, which constitutes us into the Body of Christ. This Body is expressed as churches in different localities. This is the subject of Romans. The *Life-study of Romans* takes this line as its center and speaks of numerous truths in a clear way. Now a life-study of the entire New Testament has been accomplished. We have to encourage the churches in every place to study the life-studies carefully, because the life-studies are full of diamonds.

For example, although we all have read Romans 8, we may not be clear concerning what it talks about. Now the *Life-study of Romans* tells us clearly that the subject of Romans 8 is that the Triune God is dispensing Himself into the tripartite man. If you could ask Martin Luther about the subject of Romans, he would tell you that Romans speaks about justification. His explanation would stop at only the first station. Hence, we all have to diligently learn the truth. This is what is meant by the Chinese saying, "Reading is always beneficial." As long as we open the life-study messages and study them every day, regardless of what chapters or verses they cover, we will profit from them.

PROPAGATING THE TRUTH TO THE HOMES AND EXPECTING THE REVIVAL OF THE CHURCH

By the Lord's grace, we have already translated the life-studies into many different languages. This is the proper way to propagate the truth. However, not only should we propagate the life-studies as literature to other countries, we should also spread them into the saints' homes. All the saints among us should have the life-studies on display everywhere in their homes, such as on the coffee table and the nightstand. In this way the atmosphere of pursuing the truth will flourish among the saints.

Today the reason that the gospel of the Lord cannot be spread is that we do not know the truth. The truth is the gospel. If we speak the truth in every place, we are in fact preaching the gospel in every place. The entire Bible is the gospel of God, but it seems that we do not understand this. Now we have to turn this situation around so that all the saints among us will know how to speak the truth and preach the gospel. This will provide the Lord a broad way to fulfill His desire.

The co-workers in particular have to be constituted to the extent that they "forget" the heavens, the earth, who they are, and how many children they have. They should know only the Bible, the life-studies, and the explanations in the footnotes in the Recovery Version of the New Testament. If there were one hundred co-workers among us who really knew the truth and who spoke it every day in the meetings and in the saints' homes, this would not only change the atmosphere of the church but would even shake the whole society. If the saints have life-study messages everywhere in their homes, their spiritual condition will be greatly revived. If they have the Lord's word, it will be impossible for them not to be revived. This kind of prospect is not hard to attain. As long as we are willing to take the lead to encourage the whole church to read and to absorb what they have read, revival will definitely come.

A FEW KEYS TO THE LEARNING OF THE TRUTH

Some people say that it is not easy to read the Word because they often forget what they have read. They also say that if they have to read the life-study messages, it will be even more difficult. What they say is not wrong; to be constituted with the truth surely requires that we pay a price. One person's way of studying, however, may be different from another's. In order to be constituted with the truth, we need to learn some secrets. Consider learning English as an example. Although I studied English for only two to three years in my youth, I had a proper method of study. As a result, I gained a great advantage in learning English. Thus, I was able to understand the English Bible. Now I can understand every English book. If there are some unfamiliar words, I only need to look them up in the dictionary. This is all because of my proper learning in my youth. It is the same with studying the truth. Every book of the Bible contains the spirit of its writer. On the one hand, we have to study the meaning of the words thoroughly; on the other hand, we have to touch the spirit of the writer.

Second, in studying the truth you cannot be isolated from others. You have to go out to visit and fellowship with the churches. There is a Chinese saying that says, "Traveling ten thousand miles is better than reading ten thousand books." Fellowship widens our horizons. For instance, if we are studying Romans, and the church in Taipei is also pursuing Romans, then we should go to visit them and receive help from them through fellowship.

Third, we have to learn to use the appropriate reference books and concordances. For example, *Strong's Exhaustive*

Concordance of the Bible has numbered and identified more than 5,600 Greek words which are used in the New Testament. At present, almost all the Bible expositors and those who pursue the truth use this book. The *Theological Dictionary of the New Testament* written by Gerhard Kittel and the New Testament word study of Henry Alford both contain deep analysis on the meaning and usage of every significant word in the New Testament. We have to know how to use these reference books. Fourth, if possible, it is best to learn Greek, which is the language in which the New Testament was written. If we can understand it, it will be very helpful in our study of the truth.

THE TRUTH ENABLING MAN
TO RECEIVE LIGHT AND FREEDOM

The Lord Jesus said that the truth shall set us free (John 8:32). There is light in the truth, and once we receive the light, we are set free. During the time of the Lord Jesus, the Pharisees and lawyers also read the Old Testament, but they studied only the letter without the light of the truth. However, once the Lord Jesus gave the explanation, the truth was revealed. For example, there was a group of Sadducees who did not believe that there was such a thing as resurrection, so they went to question the Lord. The Lord Jesus said to them that in Exodus 3:6, the section concerning the burning bush, Moses clearly pointed out that God is the God of Abraham, the God of Isaac, and the God of Jacob. The Lord also told them that God is not the God of the dead but of the living (Mark 12:18-27; Luke 20:27-38). Since God called Himself the God of Abraham, the God of Isaac, and the God of Jacob, this proves that Abraham, Isaac, and Jacob, who had died, will be resurrected. This example shows us that the Lord Jesus' knowledge of the truth and the light of the Scriptures was very thorough, and that the way He expounded the Scriptures was not only according to letter, but also according to the life and power implied within them. This is also the focus of the life-studies. Thus, we must make an effort to read the Bible and study the life-studies in order to know the truth.

We do not need to worry about the shortage of material or about the way for us to pursue the truth. The only need is for us to be willing to spend the time and effort on this matter. If we all rise up to study the truth and to know and pursue the Lord, this will bring in a big, long-lasting, and genuine revival of the church.

CHAPTER NINE

THE THIRD GREAT PILLAR
IN THE LORD'S RECOVERY—THE CHURCH

Scripture Reading: Matt. 16:18; 18:17; Acts 8:1; 9:31; 12:1;
13:1; 14:23; Rom. 16:1, 3-5a, 16, 20; 1 Cor. 12:28; Rev. 1:4-5a, 11

THE DEFINITION OF THE CHURCH

The Body of Christ

The four pillars in the Lord's recovery are the truth, life, the church, and the gospel. In the New Testament the first person is Christ and the second person is the church. Today Christians in general pay some attention to Christ, but they do not pay much attention to the church. Although they often mention the church and discuss it, in their realization the church is nothing but a building or a human organization. However, the Bible clearly shows us that the church is the Body of Christ (Eph. 1:22b-23). The church was produced by Christ, Christ is the Head of the church, and the church is the Body of Christ. A human body is not an organization but a living organism. Likewise, the church is not an organization but an organism. As believers, we are the members of this organism.

A person's body has many members, but it is still one body. The members of the body are comely and lovely and are able to receive the supply of life. However, once a member is separated from the body, not only will it lose its life and function, it will also become a dreadful member. Suppose someone cut off his own hand and gave it to you. This would scare you. However, if his hand remains attached to his body, it can warmly shake your hand. It is regrettable and terrible that many Christians today are like hands cut off from the body.

They have become individualistic members who are detached from the Body. In addition, because they are separated from the Body, they lack the life supply of the Body and lose their usefulness in the Lord's hand.

The House of God and of the Believers

The Bible also says that the church is the house of the believers (cf. Gal. 6:10). In this house, God is the Father and we are the children. Hence, this house is the house of God (Eph. 2:19; 1 Tim. 3:15; Heb. 3:6). If a person is homeless, he becomes a wanderer. Many Christians today are like homeless wanderers. They would rather be Christians "on the roadside" than children in the Father's house. Whether it is referred to as the Body of Christ or the house of God, we believers need the church. Since we are members of the Body of Christ, we must remain in the Body; since we are children in the house of God, we must stay in the house.

THE LORD'S INTENTION TO BUILD
THE REDEEMED BELIEVERS INTO THE CHURCH

The Lord's Dealing with the Believers and Perfecting of the Believers through the Church

The Bible reveals to us that the Lord's purpose in saving us is to build us into the church. Christians often say that they need to edify and build themselves up, but the Bible says that the Lord wants to build the church (Matt. 16:18). In my experience of serving the Lord for more than fifty years, I have never seen an individual Christian who was able to build himself up. The more individualistic we are, the more we are unable to build ourselves up. We can be built up only when we are in the Body, the church. When we are in ourselves, we can only cause problems. The more individualistic and peculiar a believer is, the more he will be full of the self. The more individualistic and natural he is, the more he will be full of the disposition of the self. The peculiar disposition and natural life of a Christian cannot be removed in any other place; they can only be dealt with in the church. Every member in the church is both a supply and a dealing to us.

Suppose there is a person with a quick temper who is concerned about doing everything with speed and efficiency. Even after such a one has been married for twenty-five years, his wife may still be unable to deal with his quick temper. However, once he comes to the church and is built up in the church, his quick temper is slain. He wants to be fast, but the Lord arranges a slow person to coordinate with him. Suppose there is another person who has a slow temper. His family also may have no way to deal with him. However, once he comes to the church, the Lord will have a way to make him become faster. This is really wonderful! The Lord arranges the quick ones to hasten the slow ones, and He arranges a few slow ones to deal with the quick ones.

All the married ones know that husbands do not know how to deal with wives, nor do wives know how to deal with husbands. If a husband is too harsh on his wife, she may refuse to cook or do the laundry. She may also murmur a lot. All husbands confess that none of them is capable of dealing with his wife, so as to make her a better wife. Husbands simply have no way to do this. Therefore, if a husband wants his wife to be dealt with, he has to bring her to the church. The church is the best place for her to be dealt with. In the same way, there is not one wife who can adjust her husband. The best way to adjust one's husband is to send him to the church.

The church is the best place for us to be dealt with. For example, if my feet wanted to walk but my hands were not willing to go forward, these two would have to fight and deal with one another because the feet cannot tell the hands, "Since you are uncooperative and unwilling to go forward, we should be separated." This separation would cause the feet to become dreadful feet. Today some Christians are similarly dreadful. May our eyes be opened to see this serious matter. Once we are detached from the church, we are useless and become the most dreadful persons. We have no other way or choice; our destiny is in the church. This is God's sovereign wisdom.

We stand on the ground of locality in the Lord's recovery and cannot choose a church according to our desire. Today

Christianity is like a marketplace of churches. This is not right. If you want to buy a pair of shoes that you like, you can choose between a few shoe stores; however, you cannot choose which church that you would like to go to, because there is only one church in a locality. If you complain that your local church is not good and decide that since you are not satisfied with it, you want to choose another one, you will have to move to another locality. You may move to another place, but if you have not changed, the church there will be even worse. Eventually, you may move many more times. Thus, you will become a Christian who is "on the roadside." This is very pitiful.

Hence, when we mention the church, on the one hand it is so sweet, but on the other hand it is unbearable. The first stanza of *Hymns*, #852 says, "Thy dwelling-place, O Lord, I love; / It is Thy Church so blessed." However, many people do not think this way. They may say, "O Lord, Your dwelling place is pitiful. I really cannot live there any longer. Why don't You give me a better church?" Eventually, having left the church, these ones are without a church and become wandering Christians, individualistic members. Peter is the best pattern of our need to be in the church. In Matthew 16 the Lord Jesus said to him that he was a piece of stone and that He had to build him, this piece of stone, into the church (v. 18; 1 Pet. 2:5). Peter was one who had a quick temper (Matt. 17:24-27). Only the church could deal with him and make him mature. Everyone who is as fast and wild as Peter has to be in the church in order to be transformed.

The Church Being the Gathering of the Believers and Leaving the Church Being Improper for the Believers

On the one hand, the Lord has to build the believers into the church, and on the other hand, the believers cannot leave the church. In Matthew 18 the Lord said that if a brother refuses to hear the church, let him be just like a Gentile (v. 17). This does not mean that we should excommunicate him but that because this brother does not behave properly, we cannot regard him as a brother; instead, we should regard him as a Gentile. Hence, for a believer to leave the church is a kind of punishment. For this reason, in the church we should seriously receive the dealings arranged for us by the Lord.

The Producing and the Building Up of the Church

The Lord mentions the church in the Gospel of Matthew, but the church had not yet been produced at that time (16:18; 18:17). However, as recorded in Acts, one day three thousand people were saved and then about five thousand on another day (2:41; 4:4). In chapter eight, instead of being called the believers in Jerusalem, they were called the church in Jerusalem (v. 1). In Acts 9:31; 12:1; 13:1; and 14:23, the believers in different places were called the church in those places. Chapter fourteen records that Paul went out to preach the gospel, passed through many places, and led many people to the Lord. Perhaps in less than a year Paul went back to these places and "appointed elders for them in every church" (v. 23). Those believers had been saved for no longer than a year, but the Bible still calls them the church, and there were some who became elders in the same year that they were saved.

According to our concept we tend to think that a group of newly saved people cannot be considered the church. They can only meet together, and there is no way to appoint elders from among them. How could a Christian who has been saved less than a year be an elder? However, Paul did not think this way. Right after he had preached the gospel and led some people to be saved, he came back to those places, called them churches, and appointed elders in place after place. No doubt, those churches were young churches and those elders were "baby elders."

Although we are all spiritual children when we are saved, once we start meeting and living in the church life, we spontaneously grow. The church is a place that causes us to grow. Perhaps someone will say that since he has been saved for thirty-eight years, whenever he comes to the meetings, he finds that everyone there is either a spiritual child or a young person, so he simply stays at home. However, he has never considered that if he stays at home, he will become a thirty-eight-year-old child, "an elderly infant." If we want to grow, we must remain in the church. Once a person stops meeting with the church for two or three weeks, immediately he stops growing. If he does not meet for two years, he will become like a child again. If he stops attending the meetings for another three years, he will be nearly finished in his spiritual life.

Being Able to Grow in Life Only in the Church

This is a wonderful matter. Even though the condition of the church may not be good, when people come to meet, they spontaneously grow in life. Never think that in the church meetings the message is not good enough, the sharing is not up to the standard, the singing is a mess, and that you would rather stay at home. If you do so, you will lose many blessings, and your spiritual life will wither. The principle of God's blessing is that His blessing is in the Body, the church. Hence, attending the worst church meeting is better than staying at home, because whoever becomes individualistic loses the Lord's blessing. If we want to be blessed, enjoy grace, and grow in life, we have to attend the church meetings. Even though we may just be following others to pray and sing in the meetings, we will still grow in life. For example, suppose there is a church that truly resembles the church in Laodicea; it is neither hot nor cold. When people come to the meetings, they become sluggish, wanting to rest and sleep. Even the elders doze there. However, even if this is the case, as long as we do not leave the church we will still grow in life, because God's blessing is in the church.

Some people may argue, saying, "I can read the Bible anywhere. I can come near to the Lord at home." This is true, but if you leave the church and pursue the Lord at home, your pursuit surely will not last long. You may be able to rise up at six on the first day, but on the second day you will change your rising time to 6:15. On the third day you will change it to 6:45, on the fourth day you will postpone it until 7:15, and on the fifth day, you may not get up at eight. Then on the sixth day you may not even want to come near to the Lord. Thus, it is impossible to pursue the growth in life apart from the church. The blessing is in the church. Even the weakest church is stronger than the individual.

THE BLESSING IN THE CHURCH

God Crushing Satan under the Feet of the Built Up Church

The Bible pays much attention to the church. Romans 16 tells us that there was a deaconess of the church in Cenchrea, Phoebe, who loved the church very much and served the church absolutely (v. 1). Then it also mentions a couple, Prisca and Aquila, who knew nothing but the church (v. 3). Wherever they were, they "operated" a church. When they were in Rome, they "operated" the church there, and when they went to Ephesus, they also "operated" the church there. Why do we say that they were "operating" the church? It is because wherever they went, the church in that locality would meet in their home. Because of their love toward the church, Paul said that he and all the churches of the Gentiles gave them thanks (vv. 4-5a). Many readers of the book of Romans have not seen that it concludes with the local churches. The last chapter of Romans is focused on the local churches. Only the local churches can fulfill God's purpose and deal with God's enemy. Hence, if we had been in Cenchrea, we would have had to meet with the church in Cenchrea. If we had been in Rome, we would have had to meet with the church in Rome. If we had been in Ephesus, we would have had to meet with the church in Ephesus. Only in the local churches can we allow God to have the ground to crush Satan under our feet. In other words, only when we are in the church can we overcome Satan and crush him under our feet. This is the revelation we see in the book of Romans (v. 20).

Having the Supply of the Sevenfold Intensified Spirit

In Revelation the Lord Jesus showed John that he had to write to the seven churches that grace and peace would come to them from the seven Spirits who are before His throne (1:4). The majority of Christians see only the one Spirit, but at the end of the Bible it speaks of the seven Spirits. These seven Spirits are entirely for the local churches. Hence, if we are not in a local church and do not remain in a church in a definite way, we will lose the supply of the seven Spirits. In the local church there are the seven Spirits, the sevenfold intensified Spirit, supplying the church in a sevenfold intensified way. For this reason we must see that wherever we are, what we need the most is the church in our place and that this church is the best church for us. We should never make our own choice.

THE SPECIFIC PRACTICE OF THE CHURCH LIFE— FEEDING THE LORD'S LAMBS

How then should we practice the church life? First, every saint has to nourish, take care of, and lead the new ones. In the church there are always those who are younger than we are whom we should take care of. We have baptized many people, but usually less than ten out of a hundred remain in the church. In other words, we give birth to a hundred babies, but over ninety of them disappear. What is the reason for this? It is because no one takes care of them. The saints have a wrong concept that the elders should bear the responsibility of taking care of people. However, there are only a few elders. How can they take care of so many saints? Since the church is the house of the believers, everyone in the church has to bear the responsibility of taking care of others.

Before His departure from the world, the Lord charged us to go forth and bear fruit. Once we bear fruit, the fruit will become lambs that need our care. Thus, at the end of the Gospel of John, the Lord said to Peter, "Feed My lambs" (21:15-17). Do not think that the Lord's word was only for Peter. Peter is our representative; we all have to take care of the lambs. If we preach the gospel to others, lead them to be saved, and bring them to the church to be baptized, we should not leave them alone. We have to take care of them. A mother, after giving birth to a baby, would not leave him alone. Rather, she would feed him and take care of him in a detailed way for at least eighteen years. When some people hear this word, they may feel that this is too troublesome and would dare not preach the gospel. However, please remember that before the Lord charged Peter to feed His sheep, He first asked him, "Do you love Me?" Today the Lord is asking us the same question. Do we love the Lord? Do we love His church?

There is a hymn that says, "We are for the Lord's, / We are for the Lord's, / We are for the Lord's recovery!" (*Hymns,* #1255). We all love the Lord, the church, and the Lord's recovery, yet we may not love the lambs, because feeding the lambs is a very troublesome matter. Therefore, many people say, "It is fine to ask us to preach the gospel. If a person is willing to believe in the Lord, we will bring him here to be baptized. If he is not willing, we will not force him. However, to feed him and make him a remaining fruit after his salvation will not be that easy." This is why, although everyone sings, "We are for the Lord's recovery," there is still very little multiplication and increase. This proves that in the matter of feeding the lambs, the churches are altogether unable to follow the Lord's steps and meet the Lord's standard. We cannot continue to sing, "We are for the Lord's, / We are for the Lord's recovery" if the number of saints who have stopped meeting keeps increasing year after year. We must go out to recover these saints and bring them back to the proper church life.

In the past there were thirteen to fifteen thousand saints on the name list in the church in Taipei, but only five thousand were meeting regularly. There were still eight to ten thousand who were not meeting regularly. This is abnormal. We are busy preaching the gospel and baptizing people the whole year, but after we have baptized one hundred people, ninety of them disappear in three weeks. This is not right. We should feed them. Do not say that the elders should feed them. There are only a few elders in a church; they cannot do that much. Neither should you say that all the other brothers and sisters should pick up such a burden. Each one of us has to say, "I am the one who should bear the responsibility of feeding others."

First, we have to review the information that we have gathered concerning all the saints. Then we should form every twelve people into a group, incorporating everyone into a group. We should not form the saints into groups according to their spiritual condition, nor should we assign a leading or responsible one for each group. We want every saint in each group to be responsible. Since they are in the same group, they should meet together. They can decide when and where they will meet. However, perhaps the majority of the saints in the groups may not meet regularly. It may even be the case that all the saints in the group do not meet regularly. This is the one thing that we should pay attention to. If this is the case, then we will need some full-timers to rise up and serve in coordination to take care of the saints in those groups.

THE NEED OF MORE FULL-TIME SERVING ONES

Concerning the full-timers, we need to have a kind of understanding that they are not preachers but full-time serving ones. They must spend every morning to study the Recovery Version of the New Testament, including the footnotes and cross references, and also the life-studies. They should be able to read two life-study messages in four hours each day. There are approximately 1,200 messages in the *Life-study of the New Testament*. If we read two messages each day, we will be able to read fifty messages a month and six hundred messages in twelve months. Then we will be able to read through all of them in two years.

Because most of the saints do not have sufficient knowledge of the truth, there is the need for the full-time serving ones to pick up the burden to speak the truth to people. Since the full-timers have to speak the truth, they must first equip themselves. This is different from simply giving a message on the Lord's Day. They must speak to people every day. Also, the full-timers have to help people to establish and lead the groups, and they should also speak the truth to those in the groups. Not only should the full-timers speak to them in small group meetings, but they should also speak to them individually and lead them in how to read the Recovery Version of the New Testament and the life-studies.

THE CHURCH NEEDING
TO BE FILLED WITH THE TRUTH

We should pursue the truth to such an extent that we put the life-study messages everywhere in our homes—not only in our living rooms and on the nightstands but also in the bathrooms. In this way the brothers and sisters in the Lord's recovery will develop an atmosphere of pursuing the truth. At the same time we should encourage one another not to engage in any idle talk when we visit people. Instead, we should share the truth with them. Also, when we meet each other, instead of exchanging pleasantries, we should fellowship about the truth through mutual asking and answering. Then the saints will make progress in the truth.

Today the majority of Christians, including us, may not have an adequate knowledge of the truth in general. Even some elders of the local churches cannot speak clearly concerning the difference between the titles *Jesus Christ* and *Christ Jesus*. This shows us that the degree of our understanding of the truth is too poor. Thus, we all have to learn from the very beginning. Everyone who has a heart to serve the Lord full-time must spend at least two years to study the Bible. When you go to visit people, do not speak idle words. Speak the truth. Then, gradually, you will be able to build them up and form them into a group. Then gradually everyone in the church will enjoy coming to the meetings, and everyone who comes to the meetings will study the truth and know how to speak the truth. Unconsciously, this will bring in a revival.

I really have a burden to promote the life-studies over the five continents until every saint has the life-studies at home. I believe that if every household in the churches all over the globe had the life-studies, it would take only three to five years to bring in a new revival. The Lord's word is life, power, spirit, the living water, and even the consuming fire. Today the reason why we are so cold and weak is that we do not have much of the Lord's word in us. When we enter into the life-studies and are filled with the Lord's word, we will be empowered by the Lord's word as the power and set on fire by the Lord's word as the consuming fire.

THE PROPAGATION OF
THE LORD'S RECOVERY IN THE PAST

Thirty years ago most of the churches in the Lord's recovery outside of mainland China were in Southeast Asia, including Indonesia, Singapore, Malaysia, Thailand, and the Philippines.

Together they added up to less than one hundred churches. Today there are at least five hundred and fifty churches in the world. There are over three hundred churches in the Far East; the Philippines alone has about one hundred and thirty churches. Over a hundred of them are in the southern part of the Philippines, having been raised up through getting into the sixty topics of *Crucial Truths in the Holy Scriptures*. Moreover, there are more than eighty churches in Taiwan, twenty in Japan, twenty-seven in South Korea, at least twenty in Indonesia, fifteen in Singapore and Malaysia, and around ten in Thailand. When we add up the numbers of all these churches in the Far East, it is over three hundred.

As for the churches in other continents, there are over ninety churches in the United States and more than ten churches in Canada, so there are over one hundred churches altogether. There are around sixty churches in Brazil, South America, and at least twenty to thirty churches in Mexico, adding up to around one hundred churches. So the Americas have around two hundred churches total. In addition, there are at least twenty churches in Europe, including churches in England, Germany, Belgium, Switzerland, France, Italy, Denmark, Sweden, Finland, and Spain. In Africa there are at least five countries—Ghana, Nigeria, Libya, South Africa, and Zimbabwe—that have churches, with at least fifteen churches total. Also, there are churches in New Zealand and Australia. In total, apart from the churches in the Far East, there are at least two hundred and fifty local churches in those other continents. Thus, there are five hundred and fifty churches spread over the five continents.

PROMOTING THE STUDY OF THE LIFE-STUDIES TO BRING IN A GENUINE REVIVAL IN THE LORD'S RECOVERY

We should have a burden to promote the life-studies continent by continent until every household has the life-studies, and every saint has the life-studies both inwardly and outwardly. The life-studies are for teaching and helping people to read the Bible. When you read the Bible, your mind may not be enlightened even after reading it a hundred times.

However, when you open the Recovery Version of the New Testament, there are footnotes that open the truth to you in the places you cannot understand. Once the word of the truth is opened, you will receive the revelation. Then when you read the life-studies, you will be enlightened even more. After you have read the life-studies, the few verses you have studied will be fully opened to you. Ephesians has only six chapters, but there are ninety-seven messages in the *Life-study of Ephesians*. If you read two messages a day, you will need about fifty days to finish it. After you have spent fifty days to read through all these ninety-seven messages, the content of the six chapters, the entire book of Ephesians, every sentence, and even every word will be clear and enlightening to you. In other words, Ephesians, this mysterious and marvelous book, will be fully opened to you.

OPENING THE SAINTS' HOMES BY ESTABLISHING AND LEADING THE GROUP MEETINGS

Now, based on the information that we have received concerning the saints, we should form groups of twelve and have the full-timers help the saints, not to have a Sunday service or to form a small meeting with them, but to study the truth of the Bible together. Moreover, we also have to pour out our love. If the small group is meeting at your home, you should prepare the best refreshments for them. Do not love your money, but release your money to prepare the best refreshments. I believe that those saints who do not meet regularly will be enlivened by eating these refreshments.

Furthermore, when we go to establish and lead the small groups, we should not go to the husbands first, because they are harder to deal with. Rather, we should first go to the wives, because they are usually softer and more cooperative. In many of the saved families, the husbands usually are not willing to open their homes at the beginning. However, the wives are willing, and in the end the wives influence their husbands to open their homes for the small group. Therefore, we have to contact the sisters first. Once you set them on fire, they will be burning. Then let the sisters influence their husbands. In this way the saints will open their homes one by one.

SETTING THE SAINTS ON FIRE
THROUGH THE OPENING OF THE HOMES
FOR THE PREACHING OF THE GOSPEL

The fourth pillar in the Lord's recovery is the gospel. Every saint should open his home for the preaching of the gospel. When we go to help the saints to open their homes for the preaching of the gospel, we should not replace them. Rather, we should perfect them and let them speak and preach the gospel. They may decline and say that they do not have the gift and that they do not know how to speak. At that time we have to help them. We should first speak to them and then let them speak accordingly. Experience tells us that it is through this kind of speaking that their inner being becomes burning, and the meeting becomes even more burning. Hence, the best way to recover the saints who have not met for a long time is to strongly encourage them to preach the gospel and to help them to speak the Lord's word to others. Once they begin speaking, their inner being will be burning.

We all have had the same experience. When we preach the gospel to people, our inner being is set on fire. Some people are cold inwardly because they do not speak for the Lord or preach the gospel. As long as we are willing to stand up to speak for the Lord, no matter what we speak or how we speak, we will be enlivened and even set on fire.

PERFECTING APOSTLES, PROPHETS, AND TEACHERS
THROUGH THE SMALL GROUPS

We encourage the saints to form the small groups with twelve people in each group. This is based on the Scriptures. The first small group in church history comprised the twelve apostles appointed by the Lord Jesus. It was the first small group since the dawn of history. Today we are following the pattern of the Lord Jesus to establish the saints as groups of "twelve apostles" so that the churches will be full of "apostles." First Corinthians 12:28 says, "And God has placed some in the church: first apostles, second prophets, third teachers." If we are faithful, all the saints in our locality will be apostles, prophets, and teachers in five years. Every small group will have twelve apostles, prophets, and teachers. Some people may ask, "Who would dare to say that he is an apostle?" As long as we are sent by the Lord to speak for Him and preach the gospel to our parents, relatives, friends, and neighbors, we are apostles. If we can speak more, we will become prophets. Prophets do not necessarily speak prophecies; they are those who speak for the Lord Jesus and speak Him forth. Then, we also have to teach people; in this way, we will become teachers. First, we become apostles, then prophets, and lastly, teachers. If all the saints are like this, the churches will be strong and flourishing, full of apostles, prophets, and teachers.

THE TRUTH, LIFE, THE CHURCH, AND THE GOSPEL BEING OUR PRESENT URGENT NEEDS

However, if we all have the desire to be apostles, prophets, and teachers, we must first learn the truth. If what we speak is the truth, the work of the Holy Spirit will follow our speaking. Then the words that we speak will touch our parents and friends, and they will believe and receive. After they have believed, we have to speak the deeper truths to them. Then we will become prophets, and they will know the Lord more. If we continue to speak to them for two to three years, we will become teachers, and eventually they will all know the Lord and will also speak to others. If the churches in the Lord's recovery are full of this kind of speaking and teaching, the churches will be stronger and richer and will bring forth the multiplication and increase.

Therefore, we need the truth, life, the church, and the preaching of the gospel. We also need for everyone to rise up to be an apostle, a prophet, and a teacher. In this way the church will be strong, rich, and victorious. May God bless us in receiving such a word.

CHAPTER TEN

THE FOURTH GREAT PILLAR
IN THE LORD'S RECOVERY—THE GOSPEL

Scripture Reading: Rom. 1:14-15; 1 Cor. 9:16-17; 2 Tim. 4:2a; Acts 6:4; 5:42; 10:24

THE COMPLETE AND FULL GOSPEL OF GOD

The four pillars in the Lord's recovery are the truth, life, the church, and the gospel. The truth brings us life, life produces the church, and the church is responsible for the preaching of the gospel.

Christians today have a very superficial view of the gospel. They think that the gospel tells people that they are sinners and will perish after death but that God loved the world and gave His only begotten Son to save them—He was crucified to bear the sin of the world—so that if they repent and believe in Him, they will not perish but will have eternal life and enjoy peace in the future, and they will also enjoy prosperity and peace in this age. We cannot say that this kind of a gospel is wrong, but it is superficial and very poor.

The book of Romans, written by the apostle Paul, consists of sixteen chapters, and each chapter contains the gospel. In 1:14-15 Paul says that he is a debtor both to Greeks and to barbarians, both to wise and to foolish, and that, for his part, he is ready to announce the gospel to the Gentiles. In the gospel Paul preached, which is the whole book of Romans, there is no mention of perdition, heaven, or prosperity and peace. Instead, Paul first speaks of justification, then sanctification, then the Body of Christ, and last of the local churches in every place. This means that even the local churches are a part of the gospel.

We must see that if what we preach is merely about escaping perdition and going to "heaven," then we are preaching the poorest gospel. We must preach the gospel in a way that allows people to clearly see that once they believe in the Lord, their sins will be forgiven, and they will be redeemed and justified by God, reconciled to God, and accepted by God. They should also see that at the same time they will be regenerated in their spirit, have God's life and nature, and have God dwelling in their spirit to renew them day by day and transform them moment by moment. This is so that they may be conformed to the image of His Son and eventually reach the maturity in life and be fully glorified as the sons of God. Furthermore, they should see that although they are sinners, they will become sons of God. At the same time, they are members of Christ, coordinating together to constitute the Body of Christ, which is the testimony, the riches, and the expression of Christ expressed practically on the earth as the local churches. This is the gospel in Romans.

In the New Testament there are not only the four Gospels of Matthew, Mark, Luke, and John but also the gospels of Acts and Romans. In Romans 1 Paul tells us that he preached this book as the gospel to the Romans, the Gentiles. This book is concerning the complete gospel of God, beginning with forgiveness of sins, passing through sanctification, transformation, and the constitution of the Body of Christ, and eventually arriving at the living of the church life in the churches.

Romans 8 is the center of Paul's gospel, which is concerning the Triune God dispensing Himself into the tripartite man. Hence, in this chapter Paul mentions the Father, the Son, and the Spirit (vv. 9-11). God is the Triune God—the Father, the Son, and the Spirit—for the purpose of dispensing Himself into man. We human beings are tripartite, having a spirit, soul, and body. Our mind occupies a great part of our soul. Romans 8 tells us that the Triune God first enters into our spirit (v. 10), then saturates our mind from our spirit, that is, enters into our soul (v. 6), and then enters into our body, giving life to our mortal bodies (v. 11). In this way, our tripartite being—our spirit, soul, and body—is filled with God. This is the center of Romans 8 and of the entire book of Romans as well. This is the gospel of God.

Do not think that the gospel is one thing and that the truth is another thing. The truth is the gospel, and our preaching of the truth is the preaching of the gospel. To preach the gospel is not to tell people about escaping perdition and going to heaven nor to tell them about prosperity and peace. It is to tell people about God, about Christ Jesus, and about the church. In other words, to preach the gospel is to tell people that God wants to enter into man and make sinners sons of God, that these sons of God are living members of Christ for the constitution of the church, and that these ones are in the church, which is expressed in different localities, so that they can live the church life in the local churches.

THE TRUTH BEING THE GOSPEL

Unfortunately, today most Christians have a mistaken view concerning the gospel. Their view of the gospel is too superficial and limited. Sometimes we make a distinction between the meetings for gospel preaching and the meetings for preaching the truth. When we are in a gospel meeting, we spontaneously preach the gospel, and when we are in an edification meeting, we preach the truth. Actually, this is altogether wrong, because the truth is the gospel.

Take the Gospel of John for example. This Gospel begins with God: "In the beginning was the Word, and the Word was with God, and the Word was God....In Him was life, and the life was the light of men....And the Word became flesh and tabernacled among us (and we beheld His glory, glory as of the only Begotten from the Father), full of grace and reality....For of His fullness we have all received, and grace upon grace....No one has ever seen God; the only begotten Son, who is in the bosom of the Father, He has declared Him" (1:1, 4, 14, 16, 18). This is the gospel we should preach.

In their preaching of the gospel, many people do not have the boldness to preach "In the beginning was the Word" as John did, because they do not know the truth. What is the meaning of *the beginning*? Not only are those who listen to the gospel unable to understand this, even those who preach the gospel do not know what this means. Moreover, in the Chinese Union Version, *Word* is rendered as *truth*. Then what is truth? Confucius said, "Truth is something so valuable that one is willing to die soon after learning it." Is this "truth" the same as *the Word* mentioned in John? If not, then what is the Word? The Gospel of John begins with, "In the beginning was the Word, and the Word was with God, and the Word was God....In Him was life, and the life was the light of men....And the Word became flesh and tabernacled among us...full of grace and reality" (vv. 1, 4, 14). It may seem that people will not be able to understand the truth, but we cannot say that they will not understand any of it. John knew a secret—the secret that as long as he continued to speak, people would eventually understand.

THE SECRET TO PREACHING THE GOSPEL

Let us use an illustration. When parents teach their child to speak, they do not care whether he understands or not; they simply speak to him every day. Although the child may not understand at the very beginning, as long as the parents continue to speak to him, he will gradually understand in less than a year. Perhaps he will first learn to say, "Mom," then, "Dad." The parents do not need to tell him particularly that this is dad and that is mom. He spontaneously knows whom to call. After some time he may learn to say, "Love Mom!" How does he learn to speak? It is through constant hearing. Those who are dumb are usually deaf as well. Being deaf, they cannot hear and therefore cannot speak. Thus, they become dumb.

Therefore, when we preach the gospel, we need to have the faith and boldness to speak God's word to people. Do not worry about whether they will understand or not. As long as they can hear, it will be all right. We should simply tell people, "In the beginning was the Word, and the Word was with God, and the Word was God." People may not understand it the first or second time, or even after seven or eight more times, but eventually they will understand. For example, those in the Lord's recovery always use new terminology to speak the new language, such as *the Spirit* and *the Triune*

God dispensing Himself into man. The elderly saints can testify that it is the younger ones who learn these things first. Then the younger ones speak these things to them all the time, and eventually after hearing these things many times, the older ones also learn them. This is just like the elderly Chinese people who live in the United States and learn to speak a few simple English sentences after hearing their grandchildren speak English.

Therefore, the young people need to have the boldness to endeavor to speak the truth. First you have to speak to your parents. You can tell them, "I know more than you do concerning the truths in the Bible. I know about the essential Spirit and the economical Spirit; I also know that Christ's humanity is mingled with divinity, that Christ's divinity is mingled with humanity, and that the Triune God is dispensing Himself into the tripartite man. I will speak these things to you every day; then eventually you will understand and be able to speak them as well." What a blessing of life this would bring to your parents!

From now on we should not preach the shallow and superficial gospel. We have to preach the high and mysterious gospel. Perhaps it will not be easy for people to understand, but inwardly they will appreciate and respect it. Once they appreciate and respect it, they will easily open their hearts. The problem of our gospel preaching is not in people's inability to understand our preaching but in our inability to preach. The problem is not that people cannot understand our preaching but that we only preach the superficial gospel. If we preach the high gospel, we do not need to worry about people being unable to understand or believe. In actuality, the problem is not that people cannot understand but that we do not know how to preach.

LEARNING THE MYSTERY OF THE TRUTH
FOR THE PREACHING OF THE HIGH GOSPEL

For the preaching of the high gospel, we have a strong burden to encourage everyone to pursue the knowledge of the truth. In Texas there are some saints who put the life-studies everywhere in their home—not only in the study, the living room, and the kitchen, but also in the bathroom. They make good use of their time to pursue the truth. Some saints play message tapes in their cars and listen to them while driving. We must have this kind of pursuing spirit in order to know the truth thoroughly. The truth is the gospel. This corresponds to the Chinese saying, "What is real in a person will be manifested outwardly." If we are filled with the truth inwardly, we will spontaneously express it outwardly by speaking the mystery of the gospel to people. May we all one day be able to speak the life-study messages even in our dreams. This would prove that the life-studies have been received and thoroughly constituted into us, because what we dream about at night is what we think about during the day.

We all have the heart to preach the gospel, but if we do not know the truth, we will quickly run out of words as soon as we open our mouths to speak to people. After two or three sentences we will not know what to say. In the end, we will have nothing to say, and people will be unwilling to listen to us. Hence, we must learn the truth. The word of the gospel is the truth. For us to speak the word of the truth, we must first learn the truth. If from now on we would be willing to seriously learn the truth, we all would know how to preach the gospel in two months. To preach the gospel is actually to speak the truth, because the real gospel preaching is the speaking of the truth. To speak the truth is to preach the gospel; thus, we all must learn the truth in a proper way.

THE TRUTH BEING THE URGENT NEED TODAY

Today the truth is needed everywhere. Not only the non-Christians do not know the truth; even many Christians do not know the truth. However, the Lord has given us many rich truths. Even our gospel hymns are full of precious truths. For example, the first stanza of *Hymns,* #1058 says, "Rock of Ages, cleft for me, / Let me hide myself in Thee; / Let the water and the blood, / From Thy riven side which flowed, / Be of sin the double cure, / Save me from its guilt and power." Here it mentions *the water and the blood, the double cure,* and *guilt and power.* Even many saints among us may not know the meanings of these phrases. Here the double cure refers to the cure of our outward sinful acts and our inward sinful nature. The blood refers to the precious blood shed by the Lord to deal with our outward sinful acts (John 1:29; Heb. 9:22), and the water refers to the life imparted by the Lord to deal with our inward sinful nature (John 19:34). The precious blood of the Lord redeems us from the eternal punishment we deserve due to our sinful acts, and His life saves us from the power of our sinful nature.

If we have a thorough understanding of this hymn, we will be able to preach the high gospel to people. We may invite someone to sing this hymn with us and then explain it to him. This would be a very good gospel message. After hearing this, he will be surprised and will respect the excellence and mysteriousness of the content of the gospel. When we speak to him, the Holy Spirit will work in him. Then we could sing this hymn with him again. In this way, he would probably be saved in less than half an hour. We should not say anything about perdition and "heaven" or even prosperity and peace. Instead, we should speak only about Christ Jesus, the Rock of Ages, who was crucified for us, and out from whose riven side came blood for redeeming us from the eternal punishment that we deserved due to our sins, and water for saving us out of the power of sin. This kind of simple but excellent singing and speaking, matched by the working of the Holy Spirit, will lead people to salvation. This is the proper way to preach the gospel today.

First Timothy 3:15b says, "The church...the pillar and base of the truth." This indicates that without the truth, there would be no church. The truth brings in life, and once we have life, we become the church. In addition, the unique commission of the church today is to preach the gospel, the content of which is the truth. The truth tells us one central point: the Triune God—the Father, the Son, and the Spirit—is dispensing Himself into us—sinful, tripartite men—that our sins may be forgiven and that we may receive God's life and have God Himself in us for our transformation into the sons of God. This is the truth and the gospel. We must learn the truth.

OUR COOPERATION BY PRAYER

Once we have learned the truth, we have to go out to preach. However, before we go out to speak, we must pray. The proper sequence is first to pray and then to preach. Merely having the truth without the Spirit does not work. Once we have the truth, we also have to pray that we may be filled with the Spirit inwardly. Otherwise, we will be like a flat tire, without the strength to move. In Acts 6:4 Peter said, "We will continue steadfastly in prayer and in the ministry of the word." This indicates that prayer precedes preaching. We must continually pray for those who are in our hearts—our relatives, friends, and neighbors who are surrounding us. Once we pray, we will be filled and saturated with the Spirit. With the truth and the infilling of the Holy Spirit, we will be equipped to go out to preach the gospel to others.

THE SPECIFIC PRACTICAL STEPS
FOR THE SPREADING OF THE GOSPEL

Opening Our Homes
for the Preaching of the Gospel

We have to encourage all the saints, no matter what their situation, to open their homes for the gospel. We even have to motivate the saints who are weak and the saints who have not been meeting for a long time to open their homes. This is a tremendous task, and it requires the responsible brothers and full-timers to put in all their effort. If a church has over one hundred open homes, and every home preaches the gospel at least once a week, the number of people will be doubled in just half a year. This will not only recover those saints who have not been meeting for a long time but will also cause their unsaved family members, friends, neighbors, class-mates, and colleagues to be saved through hearing and believing the gospel.

In the Bible the best pattern of home gospel preaching is seen in the house of Cornelius. Not only he himself was saved, but he also brought his whole household to be saved. When the angel told him, "And now send men to Joppa and send for a certain Simon, who is surnamed Peter," he immediately sent people to Joppa and called together his relatives and intimate friends to his house (Acts 10:5-8, 24-27). This is why when Peter entered his house, not only was his family there but also his relatives and intimate friends. This is a good pattern showing that while we are the mouthpieces for preaching the gospel, our homes are the outlets for preaching the gospel.

We must preach the gospel through our homes. The best way to invite people to your home is to invite them for meals or to prepare the best refreshments for them. When the best refreshments get into their stomachs, their hearts will be opened. As long as the best refreshments can get into their stomachs, the Lord Jesus will gain an excellent opportunity to come into their spirits. How worthwhile and meaningful this is!

The first stanza and chorus of *Hymns,* #921 say, "Rescue the perishing, / Care for the dying, / Snatch them in pity from sin and the grave; / Weep o'er the erring one, / Lift up the fallen, / Tell them of Jesus the mighty to save. / Rescue the perishing, / Care for the dying; / Jesus is merciful, / Jesus will save." As long as we are willing to open our homes, prepare the best refreshments, and invite our relatives and friends to come, they surely will be saved. This is the best way to preach the gospel. I hope that from now on, every saint would open his home for the preaching of the gospel, and every saint's home would be a gospel station for the preaching of the gospel once a week or at least once every two weeks.

Preaching the Gospel on the Campuses

Moreover, owing to the universality of education, there are many schools in many different places. The campuses are like fishponds, and the students are like the fish. All the "fish" have been gathered in the "fishponds," so we must go to every college, high school, and elementary school to preach the gospel. This requires some specific ones in every church to receive the burden to serve in the gospel on the campuses and seek all kinds of opportunities to go to the campuses to preach the gospel. On the other hand, this also requires a large number of full-timers to be raised up, especially the full-timers who have just graduated from college, because it is easy for them to go to the college campuses to preach the gospel to the college students. This is why we encourage the saints who are in school to consecrate two years after college to serve the Lord full-time. If the full-timers really have the burden to continue to preach the gospel at the colleges, this would be another profitable way to preach the gospel.

Preaching the Gospel to the Children

The third way of gospel preaching is to preach the gospel to the children. This requires the sisters to pick up the burden. It is not necessary to use the meeting hall as the place for the gospel meeting. Rather, it is best to meet at the saints' homes. Use the weekends to gather the children from your neighborhood and to invite the children of your relatives and friends to your home. Many times parents are saved through their children, so do not overlook the children's work. If, starting from now, we use our effort to work on the gospel for children whose ages range from six to twelve, then after ten or twelve years, they will be those who will rise up to bear the responsibility of the church service. This way may seem slow, but it is actually very fast. This way is also profitable.

Preaching the Gospel to People of All Levels

The fourth way is to preach the gospel to people of all levels. Most of our brothers and sisters work in different professions, trades, and circles; they may be in schools, hospitals, factories, corporations, government bureaus, or private organizations. Wherever we are, we should exercise our influence by preaching the gospel to everyone whom we contact.

THE GOSPEL BEING
THE WAY FOR THE LORD TO GO FORTH

If we preach the gospel in these four ways simultaneously, it will not be difficult to double the number of the people in the churches in a year. If all of us would rise up to learn the truth, pursue the growth in life, live the normal church life, and preach the truth as the gospel, one year later every brother and sister will be strong, and the churches will also be enriched and fruitful. Not only will the number be doubled, but the meeting also will not be short of flavor and riches. May we all receive this burden and practice accordingly in every place, leading the saints to learn the truth in a serious way and encouraging them to pursue the growth in life, to go out to preach the gospel, and to bring people to the Lord and into the church. This will allow the Lord to have a way to go forth and will also bring Him back.

About the Author

Witness Lee was born in 1905 in northern China and raised in a Christian family. At age 19 he was fully captured for Christ and immediately consecrated himself to preach the gospel for the rest of his life. Early in his service, he met Watchman Nee, a renowned preacher, teacher, and writer. Witness Lee labored together with Watchman Nee under his direction. In 1934 Watchman Nee entrusted Witness Lee with the responsibility for his publication operation, called the Shanghai Gospel Bookroom.

Prior to the Communist takeover in 1949, Witness Lee was sent by Watchman Nee and his other co-workers to Taiwan to ensure that the things delivered to them by the Lord would not be lost. Watchman Nee instructed Witness Lee to continue the former's publishing operation abroad as the Taiwan Gospel Bookroom, which has been publicly recognized as the publisher of Watchman Nee's works outside China. Witness Lee's work in Taiwan manifested the Lord's abundant blessing. From a mere 350 believers, newly fled from the mainland, the churches in Taiwan grew to 20,000 in five years.

In 1962 Witness Lee felt led of the Lord to come to the United States, and he began to minister in Los Angeles. During his 35 years of service in the U.S., he ministered in weekly meetings and weekend conferences, delivering several thousand spoken messages. Much of his speaking has since been published as over 400 titles. Many of these have been translated into over fourteen languages. He gave his last public conference in February 1997 at the age of 91.

He leaves behind a prolific presentation of the truth in the Bible. His major work, *Life-study of the Bible,* comprises over 25,000 pages of commentary on every book of the Bible from the perspective of the believers' enjoyment and experience of God's divine life in Christ through the Holy Spirit. Witness Lee was the chief editor of a new translation of the New Testament into Chinese called the Recovery Version and directed the translation of the same into English. The Recovery Version also appears in a number of other languages. He provided an extensive body of footnotes, outlines, and spiritual cross references. A radio broadcast of his messages can be heard on Christian radio stations in the United States. In 1965 Witness Lee founded Living Stream Ministry, a non-profit corporation, located in Anaheim, California, which officially presents his and Watchman Nee's ministry.

Witness Lee's ministry emphasizes the experience of Christ as life and the practical oneness of the believers as the Body of Christ. Stressing the importance of attending to both these matters, he led the churches under his care to grow in Christian life and function. He was unbending in his conviction that God's goal is not narrow sectarianism but the Body of Christ. In time, believers began to meet simply as the church in their localities in response to this conviction. In recent years a number of new churches have been raised up in Russia and in many European countries.

OTHER BOOKS PUBLISHED BY
Living Stream Ministry

Titles by Witness Lee:

Abraham—Called by God	978-0-7363-0359-0
The Experience of Life	978-0-87083-417-2
The Knowledge of Life	978-0-87083-419-6
The Tree of Life	978-0-87083-300-7
The Economy of God	978-0-87083-415-8
The Divine Economy	978-0-87083-268-0
God's New Testament Economy	978-0-87083-199-7
The World Situation and God's Move	978-0-87083-092-1
Christ vs. Religion	978-0-87083-010-5
The All-inclusive Christ	978-0-87083-020-4
Gospel Outlines	978-0-87083-039-6
Character	978-0-87083-322-9
The Secret of Experiencing Christ	978-0-87083-227-7
The Life and Way for the Practice of the Church Life	978-0-87083-785-2
The Basic Revelation in the Holy Scriptures	978-0-87083-105-8
The Crucial Revelation of Life in the Scriptures	978-0-87083-372-4
The Spirit with Our Spirit	978-0-87083-798-2
Christ as the Reality	978-0-87083-047-1
The Central Line of the Divine Revelation	978-0-87083-960-3
The Full Knowledge of the Word of God	978-0-87083-289-5
Watchman Nee—A Seer of the Divine Revelation ...	978-0-87083-625-1

Titles by Watchman Nee:

How to Study the Bible	978-0-7363-0407-8
God's Overcomers	978-0-7363-0433-7
The New Covenant	978-0-7363-0088-9
The Spiritual Man • 3 volumes	978-0-7363-0269-2
Authority and Submission	978-0-7363-0185-5
The Overcoming Life	978-1-57593-817-2
The Glorious Church	978-0-87083-745-6
The Prayer Ministry of the Church	978-0-87083-860-6
The Breaking of the Outer Man and the Release ...	978-1-57593-955-1
The Mystery of Christ	978-1-57593-954-4
The God of Abraham, Isaac, and Jacob	978-0-87083-932-0
The Song of Songs	978-0-87083-872-9
The Gospel of God • 2 volumes	978-1-57593-953-7
The Normal Christian Church Life	978-0-87083-027-3
The Character of the Lord's Worker	978-1-57593-322-1
The Normal Christian Faith	978-0-87083-748-7
Watchman Nee's Testimony	978-0-87083-051-8

Available at
Christian bookstores, or contact Living Stream Ministry
2431 W. La Palma Ave. • Anaheim, CA 92801
1-800-549-5164 • www.livingstream.com

Fellowship → Not to push the brother to the corner.

The more we grow, the less confidence we'll have toward our feeling.

(He doesn't just make Him and us as grape + clear water, but He is making grape juice.

) We will seek protection from the Body. Because it's hard to say ~~what's~~ what's of us and
                                                            what's of Him.

Sometimes God reveals His will to us. Yet He has His way (Sarah, not Hagar),
                        and   His timing (11 yrs later
                                                    ~~after~~ after Abraham
                                                    knows that he will
                                                    have descendants
                                                    as Jehovah blessed
                                                    him).